X

Air Travel Guide for Seniors and Disabled Passengers

Robert B. Ronald

Anthony Philbin

Adrianus D. Groenewege

Montreal, Canada

Please send all comments, suggestions, and information requests to:
www.helpmefly.com

Other queries may be forwarded to:

International Aviation Development Corporation
3460 Peel Street, Suite 1803
Montreal, Quebec, Canada H3A 2M1

Tel: (514) 874-0202, x.3577   Fax: (514) 874-2699

──────────────── N O T I C E ────────────────

DISCLAIMER. The information contained in this publication is subject
constant review in the light of changing government requirements a
regulations, and new industry standards and procedures. No purchaser or ot
reader should act on the basis of any such information without referrin
applicable laws and regulations, industry standards and procedures, and
without taking appropriate professional advice.

While every possible precaution has been taken to ensure accuracy of conte
the International Aviation Development Corporation (IADC) shall not be h
responsible for any damage or loss caused by errors, omissions, misprint
misinterpretations of the contents hereof. Furthermore, IADC expres
disclaims all and any liability to any person, whether a purchaser of
publication or not, in respect of anything done or omitted, and
consequences of anything done or omitted, by any such person in reliance
the contents of this publication.

First published in 2001

ISBN 0-9680783-2-X

Printed in Canada

tents

Contents *(continued)*

Appendices:

Introduction

This book represents a first attempt at bringing together a great deal of new and old information now available to assist air travelers with mobility and other medical concerns. We've chosen to focus the book on the needs of air travelers alone because the world of aviation is the IADC's primary area of expertise; because air travel represents a particularly unique form of public transportation; and because flying anywhere is something that travelers usually have to spend a good deal of money on. Basically we think that if you're going to have to pay a lot to fly somewhere, you should at least be able to enjoy the experience.

We've organized the *Air Travel Guide* not by disability or medical condition, but primarily by trip stage (arriving at the airport; getting through the airport; on the plane; etc.). Although this means that you may have some jumping around to do in order to find the information relevant to your condition, at the same time this structure allowed us to present your information within the context of the very important planning strategies and helpful hints that are so essential to your ultimate goal of a comfortable air travel experience.

The best way to get the most from this guide, in other words, is to give it a good first read through, covering all the trip stages, and then to refer back for the information related to your specific condition as you require it. You'll find the Air Travel Guide's index to be detailed and very helpful in this respect, and we guarantee you'll learn a few things you didn't expect to in the process.

Because the *Air Travel Guide* represents a first attempt at providing senior and disabled travelers with this type of focused resource, you may likely find that it has omitted certain points which you feel are essential, and included some which you may find superfluous or outdated. The point here is that, as air travelers actually experiencing the mobility and medical conditions covered in this book, you as its readers will always be the best critics and enhancers of its information. We encourage everyone who uses this guide to pass along your suggestions and comments to the feedback section of our *helpmefly.com* website, and in so doing help us to improve its successive editions in terms of both structure and content.

Finally, while putting together this guide it's become glaringly apparent that, despite the recent and significant increases in the number of air travelers with ability and medical concerns, there is still a tremendous shortage of research being done into your actual needs and statistics by governments and pertinent corporations. By using resources like the *Air Travel Guide* to help ensure that your rights and dignity as a disabled passenger are respected by the world's airports and airlines, it's hoped that they in turn will begin to take better notice of your ever-increasing segment of their traveling market, and that more private and public research will be sponsored to help them better understand your needs and further improve their accessible services and facilities.

'Senior' and 'Disabled'

This guide uses the term *senior* to describe an older individual that may require assistance to walk long distances, has trouble seeing clearly, follows a restrictive diet, uses prescription drugs, etc.—not generally to describe everyone over the age of 65, nor even 55 for that matter.

It seems that there isn't an ideal word in the English language to describe a person with a physical impediment or psychiatric disorder without limiting or generalizing the term, or somehow offending an individual or group. This publication uses the term *disabled* mainly because its commonly used, and it's generally intended to cover any one of a number of physical or mental conditions.

When quoting other sources (including the International Civil Aviation Organization (ICAO), the International Air Transport Association (IATA) and Airports Council International (ACI)), terms such as elderly, handicapped, incapacitated, invalid and 'persons with disabilities' may also be used for purposes of accurately reflecting specific documents. Other terms which these documents may include are: blind; sight-impaired; partially sighted; deaf; hearing-impaired; and mentally challenged.

Chapter 1:
Planning Your Trip

A problem-free trip for senior and disabled airline passengers begins at home. The best way to avoid problems en route to the airport, at the airport, or in flight is obviously to plan ahead, but also to remain especially diligent about *re-verifying* these preparations with airline and other representatives leading up to your departure.

Airlines must provide passengers with information concerning the accessible facilities and services which will or will not be available to them. This includes information concerning the airport of departure and arrival, airports enroute, as well as the aircraft itself. You should always be sure to make the appropriate inquiries of your airline depending upon your specific condition.

While planning your trip, be sure to keep a list containing the names and contact details of the airline staff members and other individuals with whom you're dealing. Should a problem arise at some later point, these contacts can then be quickly referred to.

Travel agents are very important contacts and are able to handle most queries directly, however questions relating to oxygen tanks, heart monitors, stretchers, guide dogs, etc., should be referred directly to airline and airport representatives. Often your advance special requests will somehow become so special that no one at the airline feels worthy of remembering them. It can't be stressed enough how important it is to verify and re-verify all of your pre-flight preparations, whether they have been made through your travel agent or with the airline directly.

Helpful Hint

When traveling abroad, **passengers should always carry photocopies** of their passport, tickets, travelers checks and all other important travel documentation. In the case of prescriptions, this rule also applies to domestic travel.

These copies, which should be kept separately from the originals, can tremendously facilitate replacement, etc, in the event that their counterparts are **lost or stolen**.

Travelers with any type of mobility or medical condition should also be sure to choose their travel agent very selectively, being careful to interview them at length with respect to their knowledge of accessibility and other requirements. Whenever possible, ask a friend with a condition similar to your own if they can refer a good agent.

Resolving complaints

All major airlines are now required by law to have a *Complaints Resolution Officer (CRO),* who must be immediately available (in person, or by phone) to resolve disputes occurring between the airline and any passenger with a disability. Remember that this person is there to serve you.

Reduced Mobility

Many senior passengers, who are normally quite mobile, can be greatly inconvenienced by the long walking distances within airports, or by the need to transfer from one terminal building to another.

Some airports have personnel with wheelchairs and electric carts readily available to assist these passengers, however it is always advisable to verify this availability. A travel agent or the airline can also arrange for an airline porter with a wheelchair to be waiting for passengers upon arrival at the airport.

Wheelchairs

Passengers who own a motorized wheelchair normally will not encounter any problems with mobility within the airport, but they may need assistance transferring from their wheelchair to the airplane seat. These arrangements should be made well ahead of time by your travel agent or through the airline. In general it's advisable to take the narrowest chair available to you.

If you plan to check a motorized wheelchair as baggage your primary concerns will be properly packaging the batteries for transport by air, and disassembly/assembly instructions. Airlines may *not* require you to sign any form of waiver for wheelchair damage or loss. If possible, you should plan to carry your charger and any other important chair parts with you as hand luggage. See *Boarding and Deplaning*, and *Preboarding* under *Preflight and Postflight* in Chapter 4.

Batteries—Different motorized wheelchairs use a variety of batteries or battery packs. Air travel regulations require that batteries be properly and safely stored, and you should always consult with your airline with respect to its specific battery packing requirements. If you wish to have the airline pack the batteries for you, 48-hours advance notification and 1-hour advance check-in is usually required. Airlines may *not* charge you for this service. See *Batteries* under *In Flight* in Chapter 4, and *dangerous goods in passenger baggage* in the Glossary.

Disassembly and Assembly—Instructions on how to disassemble and assemble a motorized wheelchair should be clearly written and *securely* attached to your wheelchair. Airlines *must* accept these instructions, as your wheelchair may have to be disassembled before it enters the cargo hold. When baggage is unloaded, all mobility devices are supposed to be given first priority with respect to removal and re-assembly.

Seating

Airlines and national civil aviation authorities have different rules concerning seat restrictions for senior and disabled passengers (see *Seating* under *In Flight* in Chapter 4). If a passenger's condition dictates that a specific seat is necessary, it is very important to reserve it well ahead of time.

Helpful Hint

It's advisable to **install a new wheelchair battery pack before starting your trip.**

Many airlines prefer batteries powered by **gel cells** these days, but regardless of this preference you should still plan for some customs delays at the security and check-in counters.

Sitting Behind a Bulkhead— Some conditions or situations may require passengers to reserve a seat behind a bulkhead (Fig. 1), where there is greater *seat pitch*. These include the following:

- passengers wearing a leg cast or a brace that must remain extended

- passengers who must use an oxygen tank or a ventilator

- passengers who are accompanied by a guide dog

See also *Oxygen and Respirators* under *Special Requests* in this chapter and *Oxygen* under *In Flight* in Chapter 4; as well as *Guide Dogs* in this chapter and under *In Flight* in Chapter 4.

Fig.1 - Bulkhead Seating

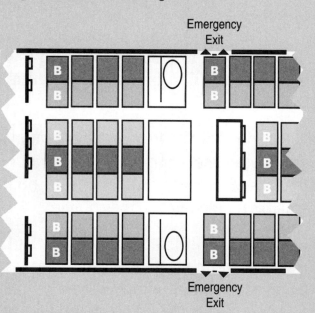

In a typical aircraft seating configuration, the seats immediately in front of an aircraft section-divider or bulkhead afford passengers greater seat pitch and leg room (marked with a 'B', left). Passengers may request these seats from their travel agent or airline when they purchase their tickets, but you should note that *bulkhead seats often don't have removable armrests.*

Seating and wheelchairs—Many passengers who require a wheelchair are able to transfer themselves from the chair to the airplane seat. This action is often made easier by removing the armrest(s) on the airplane seat. Not all airplane seats have removable armrests, but when they are available you can usually have one reserved. Passengers who are unable to transfer themselves from the wheelchair to the airplane seat can rely on the assistance of airline personnel. See *Boarding and Deplaning* under *Preflight and Postflight* in Chapter 4.

Obesity—Obese passengers may require the space of two seats and a removable armrest. They can make these special reservations through their agent or airline. It should be noted that, although policies may differ, most airlines will sell these two seats for the price of one-and-a-half, and permit a baggage allowance for two. See *Seating* under *In Flight* in Chapter 4.

Lavatories—For passengers who have difficulty walking, a seat which can be reserved close to the lavatory will be more convenient. However, it should be recognized that there will be increased pedestrian traffic and potential congestion in this location also.

On very old aircraft which do not offer an accessible lavatory, disabled passengers who can use a non-accessible lavatory with the aid of a special seat will need to provide 48-hour advance notification of this requirement to their airline.

If you are likely to experience difficulty using an aircraft lavatory, make sure your agent is aware so that they can try to arrange for a connection or stopover schedule that conforms to your personal needs. Being open and honest with your agent about incontinence and other personal conditions will help them provide you with the most comfortable travel experience possible. See also *Lavatories* under *In Flight* in Chapter 4.

Connecting Flights

On a trip that involves more than one flight with the same airline, passengers with reduced mobility can arrange, through a travel agent or the airline, for a wheelchair or electric cart to be provided for them. An airline aware that a senior or disabled passenger has a connecting flight can have an airline porter ready to escort them from their airplane seat to the arrival gate of the first flight, and to the departure gate of the connecting flight.

Arrangements to have an escort for interline flights are the same. A porter can be instructed to transport you from the arrival gate to the check-in counter of the second airline, which can have a porter waiting to escort you to the departure gate for the second airline and flight.

For a connecting or interline flight there is always the possibility of a delay between flights. If the delay between the arrival of the first flight and the departure of the second flight is minor, you should be escorted to the departure lounge of the gate of the second flight, as soon as possible. If the delay between the arrival of the first flight and the departure of the second is longer—and the gate of departure has yet to be assigned—you should be escorted to the concourse area. An airline attendant should check in on you periodically, but will not remain with you. Passengers who want or need constant attention will have to make special arrangements for a personal attendant. See *Special Requests* in this chapter and *Personal Attendants* under *In Flight* in Chapter 4.

Special Requests

Meals—Airlines provide a wide variety of meal choices based on cultural differences and health concerns. Passengers or a travel agent can check with the airline for these special meal choices. They may include meals for diabetics, as well as gluten free, high fiber, low calorie, low fat, low protein, low sodium, low purine, vegetarian and non-lactose meals. See also *Meals* and *Diabetics* under *In Flight* in Chapter 4, and Appendix 3.

Oxygen and Respirators—Passengers who require a supplemental supply of oxygen during a flight are *not* permitted to carry their own supply on board—the passenger must use the canisters provided by the airline. This must be arranged 48 hours ahead of time, by a travel agent or with the airline directly. You can transport your own supply of oxygen, but it must be stored as baggage at time of check-in and picked up upon arrival. Respirator hook-up to the aircraft's electrical supply is not a service which the airline must provide, but

Helpful Hints

*For travelers who wish to have an oxygen supply delivered to them while abroad, **The Oxygen Traveler** (tel: 937-437-6007) provides services around the world.*

*A reputable organization that supplies and makes arrangements for **personal assistants** is **Travel Aides International** (530-872-2479).*

it may do so if 48-hour advance notification is provided. A reasonable charge for this service may also apply. See also *Oxygen* under *In Flight* in Chapter 4.

Personal Attendants—Personal attendants are hired by passengers for a variety of reasons. Some passengers may need help with feeding and taking medications, while others may feel more comfortable with the attention and companionship of a fellow traveler. Certain travelers may be required by airline regulations or by law to have an attendant travel with them for medical purposes. As a result, attendants may be either a relative or a friend, or in some cases a qualified nurse or doctor. See also *Personal Attendants* under *In Flight* in Chapter 4, and Chapter 6.

Stretchers—Airlines can provide space for stretchers and stretcher patients. Two main conditions apply:

- passengers must be accompanied by at least one attendant
- a doctor's certificate must be submitted

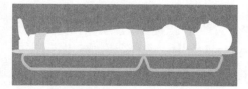

Passengers with certain types of injuries, or returning from surgery abroad, may require a stretcher. In most cases, passengers are required to use a stretcher provided by the airline. A minimum of three seats, and as many as six, must be reserved for passengers traveling on a stretcher, depending on the airline's policy and the type of airplane used. Certain airplane types *cannot* be used to transport stretcher-bound passengers. It should be noted that one extra seat must always be reserved and purchased for the attendant, whose presence is required by airline regulation or by law, and that in general 48-hour notice is required for all stretcher-related arrangements. See *Medical Clearance* in this chapter, under *Preflight and Postflight* in Chapter 4, and Chapter 6.

Guide Dogs

The use of guide dogs presents the greatest variance of rules and positions between airlines and national civil aviation authorities. For example, in the United States, there is debate among guide dog owners and guide dog organizations whether passengers should inform the airlines that they will be accompanied by a guide dog. One side argues that since it is illegal to bar anyone with a guide dog to travel in the United States, there is no need to inform anyone at the airline. The other view is that if the airline is informed ahead of time, a passenger is less likely to encounter problems. To ensure that a bulkhead seat is available, airlines should be informed at least 48 hours before a flight (see *Sitting Behind a Bulkhead* on page 5).

Passengers with a guide dog should be fully familiar with the applicable quarantine laws in foreign countries. Nations have different rules, which range from health certificate requirements to the quarantining of the dog for a period of time. In the United States, there are no travel restrictions for dogs traveling from state to state—except to Hawaii. The United Kingdom recently relaxed its mandatory six-month quarantine for dogs in order to align their policy with that of the European Union (EU).

It is recommended that any passenger planning to travel with a guide dog check applicable quarantine rules with the airline or travel agent, or where possible with the consulates of the countries concerned. This is particularly important for interline trips involving two or more airlines. For example, passengers with a guide dog can travel with airline A to site AA, but may not be allowed to travel the second leg of the trip on airline B to site BB.

Passengers with guide dogs in economy class should book a seat behind a bulkhead, where there is a greater *seat pitch* for the dog to sit/lie. There is usually ample room for a guide dog in first class, but not all airlines have first-class service, and the size of the *seat pitch* in business class varies between airlines and distances flown. See also *Sitting Behind a Bulkhead* on page 5, and *Guide Dogs* under *Preflight and Postflight* and *In Flight* in Chapter 4.

Transport of Wheelchairs and Other Equipment

It is possible to have your manual or electric wheelchair transported onto the airplane. The size of the wheelchair, whether it can fold or disassemble, and the type of airplane involved will determine whether the wheelchair can be transported on board or stored as baggage.

Helpful Hint

Onboard closets are likely only to be large enough for a single wheelchair, this space often being allocated on a first-come, first-served basis.

If you are hoping to store your wheelchair in this manner, check with your agent and reconfirm with the airline's check-in personnel to help ensure it will be available.

Some aircraft have a storage closet on board in which a folding wheelchair can be stored. Other types of equipment can be stored in the overhead compartment or under the seat if there is sufficient space. If a wheelchair or other types of medical or mobility equipment are carried as baggage, they should be stored last and unloaded first (a common practice among most airlines). All of the above should be arranged well ahead of time by a travel agent or through the airline. See also *Wheelchairs* under *In Flight* in Chapter 4.

Medical Clearance

Some passengers may require documentation from their physician stating that they are able to travel safely by air and without any extraordinary medical attention. Disability and age are *not* sufficient to warrant a medical certificate. However, some conditions warrant a medical certificate when passengers:

- are confined to a stretcher
- require oxygen or respirators during the flight
- have a communicable disease
- will likely require extraordinary medical assistance during a flight

To help make this process easier, airlines have developed their own medical forms, based on the MEDIF form and FREMEC card, developed by the International Air Transport Association (IATA) in the 1970s to facilitate air travel for senior and disabled passengers. The completed forms provide the airline with medical information that will result in you enjoying a safer and more comfortable flight. In many cases, completion of certain medical forms by a physician is required by airline regulation or law.

You can obtain the appropriate medical form(s) from your airline. See also *Oxygen and Respirators* and *Stretchers* under *Special Requests* in this chapter; *Medical Clearance* under *Preflight and Postflight*, and *Oxygen* and *Stretchers* under *In Flight* in Chapter 4; *Medical Clearance* and *Medical Forms* in Chapter 5; *Medical Clearance* under *IATA Resolution 700 and Recommended Practice 1700* in Chapter 6; and *Medical Forms & Questionnaires* in Appendix 1.

Vaccinations, Visas, and Health Insurance

It is important to check with your travel agent and airline, as well as with the consulate or embassy of the country or countries you plan to visit, for vaccination and visa requirements. See also Chapter 5, and the list of organizations that can help you find this information on-line in Appendix 2.

The potential of an illness or injury abroad that will require medical attention or hospitalization exists for everyone. Because the price of medical coverage in foreign countries can be extremely expensive, adequate health insurance must be purchased. Incidents have occurred where foreign medical institutions refused to release a patient before payment could be arranged, and those who have to

Helpful Hint

*Many policies sold as **"travel health insurance"** offer certain travel-related benefits (trip cancellation, transportation/ evacuation, etc) but not actual travel health insurance.*

When purchasing travel insurance, make careful inquiries, being sure to ask about the all-important 'pre-existing condition' clauses.

pay with their own funds may find themselves in serious financial difficulty.

The cost of medical travel insurance will increase based on the age of the buyer. Although no extra costs may be incurred due to specific conditions, e.g., heart disease, some insurance companies may refuse coverage of that specific condition and any related conditions. Passengers already enlisted in a private or work-related insurance plan should enquire if any new medical conditions developed abroad will be covered by these plans.

Preboarding

As a general principle, airlines have established preboarding procedures for seniors and disabled passengers, as well as for unaccompanied children. This applies especially to passengers in wheelchairs or walking with a cane or crutches. See also *Preboarding* under *Preflight and Postflight* in Chapter 4.

Airport and Airline Brochures and Websites

Many airports have websites and telephone information personnel who will describe the services and facilities available to senior and disabled passengers. In most cases these provide many answers for passengers, and give them a head start with potential questions to the airline and travel agent. Airlines also offer information regarding their airport check-in and in-flight services.

Packing

Packing is one of the most important steps in the planning process. The most essential items to pack properly are glasses, medications and prescriptions (see below). Other items you may wish to consider bringing along are an inflatable cushion for the flight, and extra name labels for your equipment and baggage.

Glasses—Passengers who wear glasses or contact lenses should always have a spare pair in case of loss, theft or damage. As is the case with medications, it is best to carry glasses and contact lenses as hand luggage. It is always advisable to carry a prescription.

Medications—Medications should always be carried in their original containers to avoid confusion or misunderstanding when passing through customs. Passengers should always carry enough medication to avoid having to renew a prescription during their trip. It can be difficult and time consuming to replace medications outside of the country of purchase, and in these circumstances it is important to pack sufficient medication with hand luggage. See also *Medical Clinics* in Chapter 3, and *Security and Customs and Medications* under *Preflight and Postflight* in Chapter 4.

Prescriptions—Like medications, prescriptions should be carried as hand luggage. Prescriptions written in one country

 will not be filled in a foreign country, but having a prescription from your country of residence may assist you in obtaining a new one from a physician in the country you are visiting. See also *Medical Clinics* and *Pharmacies* in Chapter 3.

Chapter 2:
Arriving at and Departing from the Airport

Advance Planning

In general, larger airports will have numerous information resources which can supply important accessibility details to senior and disabled passengers. The phone, the web, and airport brochures are usually your best bets for this type of research. It's important to note that, although you may be familiar with the layout of your local airport, the facility you're flying to can potentially harbor a number of unpleasant surprises. Try and find out as much as you can from your travel agent, your airline(s), as well as the airport(s) themselves as part of your advanced planning process.

Arriving and Departing in a Car

Most airports will have parking spaces reserved for disabled persons near the terminal. Passengers who find it difficult to walk long distances should inquire in advance about transportation resources between the parking lot and the terminal. Some airlines may have an airline employee meet the passenger in the parking lot if the parking lot has a service telephone, or if the passenger calls on their cell phone, indicating where they are parked.

Many airports have manual wheelchairs and luggage carts at parking lot entrances/exits which can be used for transport to the airline check-in desk. Arrangements can be made for an airline employee to escort a passenger within the airport (see *Transport of Passengers* in Chapter 3). Where possible, passengers should park as close as possible to their airline's check-in counter. Individual airline signs are usually well marked in the parking lot.

Arriving and Departing in a Rented Car

For disabled passengers specifically, the possibility of renting a car at one or both ends of a trip depends on the extent of their disability, the size of the airport, the cities of departure and arrival, and the

Helpful Hint

*Most European countries now honor **disabled parking** identification from the U.S. and Canada. The placards must display the international symbol for disability, and state the name of the document holder.*

availability of specialized rental cars. Some, but not many rental companies serving larger cities and airports may be able to provide a car adapted for various disabilities. This is something that you'll want to determine and arrange well ahead of time.

Arriving and Departing in a Taxi

Disabled passengers who have traveled in the past are likely to be familiar with taxi practices in their own city. However if you must rely on taxi service at your city of arrival, you should be aware whether any of the local taxi companies can accommodate you.

Taxis and Guide Dogs—Passengers with guide dogs should inquire with their travel agent, airline or airport authority regarding whether or not local taxis will serve them, or if instead they'll need to reserve a taxi from a specific company. In some countries it is illegal to refuse a ride to a person with a guide dog, but you should keep in mind that this is not always the case.

Helpful Hint

Travelers in the United States who have difficulty renting a wheelchair-accessible or scooter-accessible van should contact either **Wheelers Inc.** *(serving 29 states and the Wash. D.C. area, 800-456-1371), or* **Wheelchair Getaways** *(47 cities in 38 states, 800-642-2042).*

Other travelers should remember that they can arrange to have a porter meet them with a **wheelchair** *when they arrive at the airport.*

Taxis and Wheelchairs—When reserving a taxi, wheelchair passengers should request that the car sent by the company has a trunk large enough to hold their equipment. Owners of larger electric wheelchairs may want to reserve a station wagon or minivan to guarantee proper service. If you require help with lifting your wheelchair and moving to and from the taxi seat, it's important to indicate to the cab company that your driver will be expected to assist you.

Taxis and Other Medical Equipment—Carrying a ventilator, prosthesis, crutches, and other equipment in a taxi should not be a concern unless the equipment in question is too large for the car. For passengers traveling on stretchers, see *Arriving and Departing by Ambulance* in this chapter.

Arriving and Departing in a Bus

Whether it is a municipal bus, a hotel shuttle, or an airport shuttle, different accessibility rules and policies exist in various cities and countries. If your travel agent is familiar with your destination they may be able to adequately advise you, but if not then you may wish to try the web or any other means at your disposal.

Arriving and Departing by Ambulance

Passengers with certain conditions of disability, passengers injured while on vacation, and passengers returning from surgery abroad may need to be transported on a stretcher. If this is the case the passenger will have to arrive at and depart from the airport in an ambulance, which requires medical clearance. See also Chapter 5.

Transport from the Parking Lot to the Terminal

Information obtained from airport authorities (see *Advance Planning* in this chapter) should advise passengers with mobility concerns of the recommended route(s) from the parking lot to the airport terminal. A passenger should be able to ascertain if elevators and ramps are present, and if wheelchairs or electric carts are available. See also *Arriving and Departing in a Car* in this chapter.

Chapter 3:
At the Airport

Airport design has changed considerably over the last 25 to 30 years. Renovations to many older facilities have made airport access for the senior or disabled passenger easier, and many new, modern airports have been designed and built keeping accessibility in mind.

In many cases the airports have evolved due to national laws that require conformity, and in some cases the airports have adapted because airport authorities are aware of the market potential of senior and disabled passengers. Still, you should never assume that *all* airports are designed to accommodate your needs. As a rule, smaller airports in remote locations are generally unlikely to have the wide range of services and facilities provided by those in larger urban centers.

It is important to always verify in advance (see Chapter 1) about your airport of arrival as well as your airport of departure. Many airports provide information resources (websites, brochures, etc.) that detail the scope and limitations of their facilities.

Airports Council International *(ACI, the world organization of airports; see Appendix 6)* has been instrumental in developing guidelines for its member airports which are intended to help improve accessibility. They offer a publication entitled *Access Travel: Airports - A Guide to the Accessibility of Terminals,* which lists the accessibility features for over 500 international airports. Readers with an interest in this topic can find ACI's technical design recommendations for airports in Appendix 5, and contact details in Appendix 6.

Stairway concerns

Airport stairways can obviously present some difficulties, especially if you happen to be carrying any heavy baggage at the time. Fortunately, the availability of elevators and escalators in virtually every airport means that very few passengers will be obliged to use a stairway in a terminal facility, and you should make sure that a resource of this type isn't available in some part of the building you're in before attempting the stairs. In the event that no elevator or escalator is available, you should be sure whenever possible to avoid circular staircases, particularly steep staircases, those with slippery steps, those without railings, and those with a large number of steps without a landing where you can rest.

Moving Walkways, Ramps and Escalators

 Major airports generally cover vast amounts of space, and passenger facilities may be separated by significant distances. Even young, fit individuals may find it exhausting to walk the long distances from the parking lot to the check-in gate, on to the boarding lounge, and finally to the aircraft.

To assist passengers in this regard, most airports have extensive networks of moving walkways, and all major facilities must now include at least one accessible route from their entrances through to the check-in, security, baggage and gate/boarding areas. In general, this route should minimize any extra distance that you're expected to travel compared to other passengers.

Stepping onto a moving walkway or escalator can be awkward for any traveler, but it is especially demanding if you happen to be using a wheelchair, crutches, or a cane. Longer walkways sometimes run on a slope, which can pose additional difficulties for wheelchair-, crutch- or cane-dependent passengers. Always exercise due caution with these devices.

Helpful Hint

*Passengers who do not require a wheelchair yet have some **difficulty walking long distances** may wish to consider the rental of a lightweight stroller-type unit for use on longer segments of their trip. **Convaid** (888-266-8243) supplies several pediatric and geriatric devices of this nature that will support passengers weighing as much as 175 lbs.*

Whereas moving walkways once posed a potential source of danger to guide dogs and their owners, most dogs are now trained to deal with these devices. Owners should make use of these mobility aids at their own discretion.

Ramps are an ideal alternative to steps, and represent the best choice for passengers using wheelchairs where elevators may not be available.

Elevators

All large airports generally have a comprehensive elevator system. All airports should have at least one elevator available to reach each level of each building, suitable for use by passengers with reduced mobility.

Signs

All travelers rely heavily on information signs that direct them to the specific facilities and services within an airport, such as entrances, lavatories, elevators, telephones, check-in counters, etc.

Senior and disabled travelers should note that signs incorporating pictographic symbols (such as those used as illustrations in this guide) may vary from country to country and even airport to airport. Whether you are using the pictograms contained in Appendix 4 of this guide, or those from any other travel reference source, it should be noted that the included pictograms are intended only as general indications of how the specific symbols or signs you are encountering or looking for may actually appear.

In general, and despite what must have been the best intentions of those designing your terminal's signage system, navigating your way through a major airport has a way of becoming confusing at times. Taking a few extra moments to clearly understand the signs you encounter can save you time and lots of unnecessary frustration.

Waiting Areas and Commercial Franchises

Most large airports have a designated concourse for stores, restaurants and shops near to the general waiting areas within the main terminal building. If a traveler encounters shops or restaurants which do not provide adequately accessible facilities for seniors and the disabled, they should bring this matter to the attention of the airport's management.

Information Desks and Check-in Counters

Most information desks and check-in counters are located close to, and clearly visible from, the main airport entrance. Counter heights will generally be at wheelchair level, and if unattended, may include a telephone. If only one or a select few counters for disabled passengers are available, they should be indicated with the international wheelchair symbol (see Appendix 4). Baggage areas will generally never have barriers such as turnstiles or gates.

Lavatories

The number of lavatory facilities found in an airport is based on the size of the airport and the number of passengers processed. Most airports will have lavatory facilities for the disabled on both sides of waiting, entrance and gate areas. The lavatory facilities are either integrated into the general facilities or located adjacent to the general facilities. The lavatories will generally be accessible from both sides of a wheelchair.

Telephones

Passengers who are blind, hard of hearing, or have speech impediments are those most likely to have problems with standard telephones. Each terminal will likely have at least one *telecommunications device for the deaf (TDD)*. All major airports generally have public telephones equipped with a hearing aid coupler coil on a handset and an amplifier, as well as a typewriter telephone. Both will have clearly worded operating instructions. Some telephones may also be equipped with a seat for senior passengers.

Medical Clinics

Larger airports employ several thousand persons who deal with tens of thousands of passengers that move through an airport daily. Needless to say, any facility that processes this many persons warrants medical facilities.

In the case of an emergency—whether minor or major—larger airports should therefore have ample medical facilities. However some smaller airports may not. Depending on your specific condition, you should always check with your travel agent or airline about the extensiveness of medical facilities available to you en route, and at your destination airport.

Pharmacies

 Most airports have at least one pharmacy. These facilities generally provide travelers with sleeping, antisickness or headache pills, but in the airport of departure they can also fill prescriptions if a traveler forgets their medication at home.

You should note that a prescription can *only* be filled within the country in which it was written. If you lose or forget a prescription or medication you can see a doctor at the airport medical clinic who in most cases can write a new prescription. Normally, these medications will have to be paid for immediately, although travelers may later be reimbursed by their travel insurance. The best way to avoid this potentially time-consuming and costly problem is to plan the trip well in advance, to carry prescriptions and medications on your person, and to ensure that you're covered by a comprehensive travel insurance policy. See *Packing,* and *Vaccinations, Visas, and Health Insurance* in Chapter 1.

Transport of Passengers

Some senior and disabled passengers may require transportation assistance within the airport. They include passengers who use their own manual wheelchairs, a manual wheelchair provided by the airline, or an electric cart driven by an airline or airport employee. Although most airports will have these services readily available, it is advisable to check ahead of time with either the airline or one's travel agent. If you have difficulty staying in your chair as you operate it, and do intend to use an airport- or airline-provided manual wheelchair, it would be wise to bring along your own belt as most airport/airline chairs will not arrive with one attached.

Blind and Sight-Impaired Passengers

The single most important barrier facing blind persons is unfamiliarity with the airport environment and facilities. A busy airport is not a familiar area, and even if the airport is designed with ease of movement for the blind passenger in mind, it is generally far from perfect.

A modern airport generally contains no obstructive furniture between an average sized adult's hip and head level, primarily because cane users are not able to identify these obstructions. Projections that do exist, such as post- or wall-mounted public telephones, normally extend to the floor itself. If not, the height of the projection's bottom end will likely allow a blind passenger's cane to touch the wall before the passenger's body strikes the projection.

Sight-impaired passengers rely on signs which are large and clear in print. The signs will usually be well-lit, and if possible, they may be complemented with audio signals.

At the Airport

Deaf and Hearing-Impaired Passengers

Visual information is vital to allow deaf passengers to be able to navigate through an airport. Signs will likely be clear, large in print, and well-lit. Airline and airport personnel should be made aware that deaf passengers who require supplementary information may rely, to a large extent, on tele-typewriter (TT) services or written communication.

Staff Training

You'll generally have to deal with a number of airline, airport, and ground handling staff while at the airport. It is obviously important that all of these personnel are well informed and well trained in order to deal with the wide range of specialized situations and requirements that may confront them. Most airport employees have been trained in dealing with senior and disabled passengers. Normally, this training includes the following:

- basic first aid
- different types of disability
- airport facilities specific to senior and disabled passengers
- how to transfer a passenger from one wheelchair to another
- how to handle different types of wheelchairs
- how to escort blind and visually-impaired passengers
- how to communicate with deaf and hard of hearing passengers
- how to communicate with speech-impaired passengers

Chapter 4:
On the Airplane

This chapter is divided into two parts: *Preflight and Postflight*, which details the importance of the check-in process, including customs, security, and baggage; and *In Flight*, which details the in-cabin time during a trip, including seating, the use of onboard wheelchairs, lavatories, and stretchers.

PREFLIGHT AND POSTFLIGHT

Check-in Counter

The check-in process should not be problematic if preparations have been made beforehand. Take advantage of the check-in process to remind the check-in agent of your requests for assistance or special requirements. No system is foolproof, and delays or tasks forgotten may occur with any airline or handling company at any airport. It is for these reasons that seniors and disabled passengers are encouraged, although not obliged, to check in earlier than the standard check-in time for a specific flight.

Baggage

Senior and disabled passengers may require transport of their wheelchair or other equipment on the flight. Rules of carriage differ from country to country and from airline to airline, but passengers should expect to be able to bring wheelchairs, canes, crutches, or respirators on board (oxygen is not permitted—see *Oxygen* under *In Flight* in this chapter). This is only possible provided that the piece of equipment can fit in the overhead compartment or under their seat, and in the case of a wheelchair does not make use of spillable batteries (see *Batteries* under *In Flight* in this chapter). Some airplanes have onboard storage closets for larger pieces of equipment.

It is important to note that the above-mentioned items are not classified as carry-on items, and therefore do not contribute to the carry-on weight allowance. For additional information see *baggage allowance, free* in the Glossary.

Airlines are expected to return stored items to the passengers in the same condition that they are checked. To ensure safe disassembly and reassembly, equipment such as wheelchairs should have clear written instructions securely attached. Airlines are *not* permitted to refuse these instructions.

Medical Clearance

Some passengers may require documentation from their physician stating that they are able to travel safely by air and without any extraordinary medical attention. Disability and age are not sufficient to warrant a medical certificate.

Airlines are entitled to demand a medical certificate if a passenger is confined to a stretcher; requires oxygen during the flight; has a communicable disease; or will likely require some other form of extraordinary medical assistance during a flight.

This process is best taken care of during the seat booking process, when you will be asked for or should volunteer your medical information to airline personnel. See *Medical Forms & Questionnaires* in Appendix 1.

Security and Customs

All passengers, including seniors and the disabled, have to clear security to board an airplane. There are some matters of importance for passengers who require a wheelchair or those using crutches or a cane. If these passengers pass through the security device without activating it, they will likely not be further screened. However, if the equipment activates the system, security personnel may decide to examine it.

If security officials deem it necessary to search wheelchair passengers, the passenger has the choice to be searched in public or private. Airport or airline security *cannot* make the decision. If a wheelchair passenger requests a private screening, a room must be provided and a search conducted within a reasonable amount of time—certainly enough to permit the passenger to reach their flight in time.

Security and Customs and Medications

For obvious reasons, *customs* officials are interested in medications carried by passengers. What is legal in one country may not be legal in other countries. Therefore, it is important to check with your doctor and your travel agent (see Chapter 5). It may be convenient to store all your medications in one container to save luggage space, but the experienced traveler will always keep each medication in its original, properly labeled container.

Passengers should always carry a copy of the prescription for each medication in case of loss, or in the case of moving through *customs*, to provide legal documentation. Few countries take illegal drug possession lightly; it is best to be well prepared. See *Medications* under *Packing* in Chapter 1, *Medical Clinics* in Chapter 3, and *Diabetics* under *In Flight* in this chapter.

Helpful Hint

All medications should be properly labeled to avoid confusion and unecessary delays at customs.

Guide Dogs

 Some countries quarantine animals upon arrival at the airport. Passengers should discuss the matter with a travel agent, airline or the consulate of the nation they intend visiting, when planning the trip. See also *Guide Dogs* under *In Flight* in this chapter, and *Guide Dogs* in Chapter 1.

Passengers with guide dogs should ensure that their animals have been adequately prepared for a long journey.

Boarding and Deplaning

Different airlines and airports use different methods to transport you from the departure lounge/gate to the airplane. Loading bridges and cross-apron buses are commonly used at large urban airports. They pose no real problems for senior and disabled passengers. Airlines provide porters to wheel you from the check-in counter to the gate and to the airplane. Arrangements for wheelchair assistance can be made in advance with the airline, by yourself or with the assistance of your travel agent.

Some airports, particularly those serving smaller cities, rely on mobile staircases which cannot be used by wheelchair and stretcher passengers, nor by people who may have difficulty climbing stairs. In such situations, airline personnel will provide the necessary assistance, and an appropriate request should be made at the time of booking, and again at check-in. If you're being transported by stretcher, special arrangements should be made well in advance.

Preboarding

Some passengers understandably feel undignified when entry onto the airplane is only possible if airline personnel carry the passenger on board. If a disabled passenger feels this way, and wishes to avoid any potential embarrassment, they can ask to be transported onto the airplane before the start of the boarding process.

Connecting Flights

For passengers traveling on more than one flight sector with the same airline or another connecting airline (referred to as *interline flights*), and requiring special assistance, a travel agent or airline can arrange for any special assistance required for the entire journey. For example, a wheelchair passenger can be escorted by a porter of airline *A* from the check-in counter of airline *A* to the gate and to the aircraft in, e.g., Boston. Upon arrival in, e.g., New York, a porter from airline *A* will escort the passenger from the airplane to the check-in counter of airline *B*, where a porter from airline *B*, who is expecting the passenger, will continue the escort to the gate of the next flight.

In larger airports where there is more than one terminal, a ground handler, employed by the airport or airline, may be involved in transportation between buildings. These are questions that can be answered by your travel agent or airline.

IN FLIGHT

Seating

Individual airlines have different policies for seating senior and disabled passengers. In some cases, availability of seating may depend on the airplane size and type. In most cases, however, the only seats that a senior or disabled passenger may *not* occupy are those in the emergency exit row, where passengers may be called upon to perform certain special duties. Passengers permitted to sit in that row must be able to:

- determine when to open the door
- open the exit door
- move quickly through the door
- devote attention to the emergency situation

Airlines can deny passengers seats in the emergency row if the passengers:

- lack mobility and strength to perform emergency tasks
- have visual problems that could affect ability to carry out emergency tasks
- are unable to communicate orally
- are unable to understand emergency instructions

Helpful Hint

*If you have the option, choose a plane that has more than 30 seats; **larger planes offer more accessibility options.** It's always advisable to inquire about your aircraft with your airline, which must advise you as to any accessibility limitations the plane may face you with (aircraft made prior to 1992 are generally less accessible than those made since).*

Air Travel Guide for Seniors and Disabled Passengers   **39**

Passengers whose conditions force them to keep their leg(s) extended; i.e., wearing a brace, leg in a cast, use a walker, etc., are unlikely to encounter any problems when sitting in first-class or long-haul business-class seats. If sitting in economy class, passengers should be seated behind a bulkhead, where the *seat pitch* is greater. See *Sitting Behind a Bulkhead* under *Seating* on page 5.

Passengers who require supplemental oxygen, or use a respirator during the flight, should make an effort to be seated behind a bulkhead, where there is ample room for the equipment.

Wheelchairs

For ease of transfer, wheelchair-bound passengers should reserve an aisle seat that has a removable armrest (see *Wheelchairs* under *Seating* in Chapter 1). Depending on the severity of your disability, you may need the assistance of airline personnel. If this is the case, you should indicate to airline personnel what is required of them, and discuss the plan of action. This may include how much physical effort will be expected of them, and

Helpful Hint

Some general tips when flying:

- *Wear comfortable clothing (the body can swell in the air)*
- *Exercise your legs, feet and toes, even while you're seated, to help prevent deep vein thrombosis*
- *Drink fluids to prevent dryness in the throat, nose, etc.*
- *Avoid alcohol and caffeine, which cause dehydration and can adversely affect your sleeping patterns*

agreement on how best to make the transfer from wheelchair to airplane seat. If you're able to transfer yourself, airline personnel should be instructed to ensure that the brakes on the wheelchair are properly activated.

You're permitted to store your wheelchair or walker in the overhead compartment or under your seat—provided it collapses or disassembles. Some aircraft have storage closets in which folding wheelchairs, including electric wheelchairs, can be stored. As a wheelchair user you have priority for the closet space as part of the preboarding process. If not, it is first come first served. See also *Batteries* in this chapter.

Lavatories

Some airplanes have onboard wheelchairs to assist you to the lavatory. It is best to check and confirm that one will be on board. For those passengers who find walking difficult over long distances and use a cane or walker, or who are unsteady on their feet, choosing a seat close to the lavatory is recommended.

All modern airplanes have lavatories built with seniors and disabled passengers in mind, but some older aircraft may pose some difficulties. You should inquire in advance about the aircraft you'll be flying on, and any accessibility deficiencies it may potentially present you with.

If and when passengers need to visit the lavatory during the flight, a flight attendant can assist them. See *Flight Attendants* in this chapter.

Guide Dogs

Passengers who are accompanied by guide dogs in economy-class seats should be seated behind a bulkhead, where there is extra room. Greater *seat pitch* will allow a guide dog to rest comfortably. Airlines differ with respect to the amount of space between seats in business-class sections. Whereas on most long-haul flights there is ample room for you and your dog, on short-haul flights business-class sections are fairly compact.

Stretchers

A passenger with a permanent physical condition, temporary injury, or under sedation before or after major surgery may require transport by stretcher. All passengers who travel by stretcher require clearance from a physician (see Chapter 5) and the in-flight presence of an attendant. See also *Personal Attendants* in this chapter, and *Personal Attendants* under *Special Requests* in Chapter 1.

Stretchers are generally secured atop three sets of rows of two or three seats, occupying a large space, and some smaller airplanes may not be capable of accommodating these needs. An attendant must always be provided with a seat next to the stretcher-bound passenger.

Diabetics

Diabetic passengers can arrange to have a special meal provided 48 hours in advance, and have a flight attendant store insulin in the cabin refrigerator. Insulin should always be with your hand luggage—never stored in baggage, in case your goods are lost or delayed.

Helpful Hint

*If you are a diabetic and uncomfortable requesting assistance from the flight crew, **insulin** can be chilled and stored in a thermos rather than the cabin refrigerator.*

Carrying syringes and vials of insulin can sometimes be a source of embarrassment and/or confusion at airport security checks. To ease a potentially uncomfortable situation, carry a letter from your physician which states that your medical condition necessitates the carriage of syringes.

Delayed flights and change of time zones can affect a diabetic passenger's control. Therefore, diabetic passengers should be sure to carry some extra food on board in case of hypoglycemic reactions.

Personal Attendants

Personal attendants can make a trip much easier and less stressful for passengers with more severe medical conditions or mobility problems. For some conditions, it is *mandatory* to have an attendant present. These include:

- passengers on stretchers
- passengers who are unable to understand safety instructions due to mental disability
- passengers whose mobility impairment is severe enough to prevent their own evacuation of the airplane during an emergency
- passengers whose hearing or sight impairment is severe enough to prevent their own evacuation of the airplane during an emergency

If you require, or choose to have an attendant present during the flight, the attendant can be a member of the family or a professional attendant, whose services can be purchased through a travel agent, an airline, or directly through an attendant agency (see *Personal Attendants* under *Special Requests* in Chapter 1). The severity of a passenger's condition will determine the attendant chosen. Passengers who need help administering medications may be escorted by a relative; passengers who require constant medical attention should require the escort of a nurse or doctor. See also Chapter 5.

Attendants must always be assigned a seat next to the passenger in question, and are responsible for helping the passenger safely evacuate the airplane during an emergency.

Oxygen

Airlines will *not* permit you to carry a personal oxygen supply on board an airplane. You can have your own supply of oxygen transported as checked baggage, but *only* the airline's oxygen canisters may be used during a flight. This must be arranged with the airline or a travel agent at least 48 hours ahead of time, and a fee may be charged.

To avoid the encumbrance of pushing or carrying the oxygen canister to the lavatory, you should bring extra tubing and connectors onto the airplane. This will allow you to have access to your oxygen in the lavatory, while the canister itself remains near your seat. See *Oxygen and Respirators* under *Special Requests,* and *Sitting Behind a Bulkhead* under *Seating* in Chapter 1.

Batteries

Electric wheelchairs use spillable and non-spillable batteries. The former must be handled with great care. If a wheelchair is securely stored in an *upright* position, either in an onboard closet or in cargo, the batteries can be left as they are. If the wheelchair cannot be stored securely in an upright position, the batteries must be removed and packaged by the airline. Non-spillable batteries are safe, but are sometimes removed by over zealous airline personnel. To avoid this inconvenience and guarantee that non-spillable batteries are not removed from a wheelchair, the batteries should be posted with a sticker clearly indicating that the batteries are non-spillable. See also *Batteries* under *Motorized Wheelchairs* in Chapter 1.

Meals

Most airlines provide a wide variety of dietary meals, including diabetic, gluten free, high fiber, low calorie, low fat, low protein, low sodium, non-lactose, low purine, and vegetarian. Since the meals have to be prepared ahead of time, it is necessary to inform the airline or your travel agent at the time of booking, or a minimum of 48 hours in advance of flight departure. See also *Diabetics* under *In Flight* in this chapter, and Appendix 3.

Flight Attendant Services

All travelers rely on the assistance of flight attendants during their trip, especially seniors and disabled passengers. Quality of service varies from airline to airline, but you should generally expect an attendant to:

- help transfer from wheelchair to airplane seat during boarding process and airplane seat to wheelchair during deplaning process

- help open food packages and identify the various foods

- assist passengers who do not require wheelchair assistance, but require help walking to the lavatory

- load and unload wheelchairs or other equipment stored on board

(continued)

- store medications, e.g., insulin, in the cabin refrigerator that require cooling during long-haul flights

In general, flight attendants are *not* required to assist you inside a lavatory, to administer your medication, or to feed you.

Chapter 5:
When You Require a Physician

Some passengers rely on a physician to provide written clearance to travel by air, obtain a prescription for medication, or to be vaccinated for some diseases such as yellow fever and cholera (a health requirement for <u>all</u> travelers visiting certain countries). It should also be noted that airlines and travel agents are able to provide detailed information regarding international inoculations and other health requirements.

There are many conditions that should not normally have a bearing on your ability to travel by air. Persons with high blood pressure, diabetes, and asthma—if properly treated—can travel with ease. Persons with cardiovascular problems should not be affected by the flight itself, but could aggravate their condition if they have to exert themselves across long distances through the airport. Some airlines now carry onboard defibrillators to assist passengers experiencing cardiovascular discomfort, but as a general guideline anyone with a medical condition should consult their doctor before traveling. Here are a few guidelines regarding some specific medical conditions:

Ear Problems— If you are suffering from sinusitis or an infection of the middle ear, significant pain and even a popped ear drum can result from changes in aircraft cabin pressure. You should not fly until your condition has improved.

Stroke— So long as your symptoms have stabilized, you are generally permitted to travel three days following a stroke.

Epilepsy— Though it does not cause any significant difficulties, some airlines may restrict travel shortly (within 24 hours) after a 'grand mal' fit.

Medical Clearance

There are also situations in which passengers must have clearance from a physician. These include:

Stretchers— Passengers who must travel by stretcher because of a permanent condition or an injury suffered while on vacation, or passengers going to or from surgery

Helpful Hint

For a list of English-speaking physicians throughout the world (125 countries), who will visit your hotel, write the International Association for Medical Assistance to Travelers at 417 Center St., Lewiston, NY 14092. Phone: (716) 754-4883

abroad, must have permission of a physician to travel by air. Without it, airlines will *not* accept said passengers. See also *Arriving and Departing by Ambulance* in Chapter 2 and *Stretchers* under *In Flight* in Chapter 4.

Oxygen— Due to the potential danger using passengers' unknown and unchecked oxygen canisters, airlines insist that passengers use canisters provided by the airlines. The airlines also insist on medical clearance from a physician if there is a request for oxygen during the flight. See also *Oxygen and Respirators* under *Special Requests* in Chapter 1, and *Oxygen* under *In Flight* in Chapter 4.

Communicable Disease or Infection— Airlines have the right to refuse carriage of a passenger if the airlines fear that the passenger suffers from a disease that is actively contagious and communicable.

Extraordinary Medical Condition— There are three general categories of passengers in this situation: 1) passengers whose conditions are likely to be aggravated during the flight; 2) passengers unable to care for themselves without special assistance not normally provided during the flight; and 3) passengers whose conditions make them a potential hazard to the safety or punctuality of a flight.

Medical Forms

Given the potential problems of misunderstanding and misinformation that a simple letter from a physician can cause, the International Air Transport Association (IATA) issued two forms, the MEDIF and the FREMEC, to make the transfer of information between physicians, passengers, ticket agents, travel agents and airlines easier and less prone to error.

It should be noted that these forms are intended as guidelines for the world's airlines, and that while some smaller airlines still make use of the actual MEDIF and FREMEC forms, most larger airlines produce their own forms or have special reservations procedures which substitute for them. Travel agents and airlines can advise you on the specific procedures to be followed.

For an overview of the types of information you should have prepared prior to filling in an airline medical form, or to assist you in answering a reservation agent's questions over the phone, please refer to Appendix 1.

Advance Notification

Most airlines require at least 48-hours notice to accommodate special requests. Some requests, such as ambulance transport and stretcher reservation may demand more time. It is recommended to make any special requests with a travel agent and/or airline and physician well ahead of time.

Prescriptions

Passengers who take prescription medicine should always ensure that their prescription is up-to-date before proceeding on a trip. Prescription medication is commonly used by senior and disabled passengers, and should be carried with the passenger. See also *Prescriptions* under *Packing* in Chapter 1, *Medical Clinics* and *Pharmacies* in Chapter 3 and *Medical Clearance, Security and Customs*, and *Security and Customs and Medications* under *Preflight and Postflight* in Chapter 4.

Chapter 6:
Your Rights as a Senior or Disabled Passenger

Laws concerning the rights of senior and disabled passengers, and the responsibilities and rights of the airlines and airport authorities, have evolved at a different pace at national and international levels. In recent decades, very important national and international legal documents and sets of industry standards concerning disabled air travel passengers have been implemented. They include the *U.S. Air Carrier Access Act (ACAA)*, ICAO's *Access to Air Transport by Persons with Disabilities*, IATA's *Acceptance and Carriage of Incapacitated Passengers*, and the IATA *Passenger Conditions of Carriage and Contract*.

The following descriptions detail the highlights of each document, and those most likely to affect senior and disabled passengers traveling by air.

AIR CARRIER ACCESS ACT

Introduced by the United States federal government in 1986, the *Air Carrier Access Act (ACAA)* was designed to help eliminate the hindrances, barriers, and discrimination that senior and disabled air passengers face at airports and in flight. The ACAA affects all United States airlines and all airport facilities within the United States, its territories, possessions and commonwealths.

Airport Accessibility

The ACAA states that all airport terminals—including parking and ground transportation—owned, leased, or operated by an air carrier, must be accessible. All facilities designed and/or constructed after 5 April 1990 must be accessible to disabled persons. New terminals must allow disabled passengers to easily access the ticketing area, and easily move between the gate and the aircraft; baggage areas must be barrier-free; and every terminal building must have a clearly marked *telecommunications device for the deaf (TDD)*.

Seating

Airlines are *not* permitted to exclude disabled passengers from sitting in an exit row, unless said passengers are unable to comply with Federal Aviation Administration

(FAA) safety regulations. Passengers who sit in emergency rows must be able to:

- locate the door and follow oral and/or written instructions
- ascertain when to open the door
- open the door
- exit quickly
- devote attention to the emergency process

Airlines may refuse a seat in an emergency row to passengers who:

- lack sufficient mobility, strength, or dexterity in both hands and arms or legs to help in the evacuation process
- are unable to read or understand emergency/evacuation instructions
- lack the ability to communicate orally
- lack visual capacity to carry out emergency/evacuation tasks

Aircraft Accessibility

All new airplanes ordered after 5 April 1990, or delivered after 5 April 1992, must comply with ACAA wheelchair accessibility provisions designed to ease some of the in-flight problems typically experienced by senior and disabled passengers.

Accessible lavatories must be provided in all airplanes with more than one aisle. The lavatory must be designed to allow passengers using an onboard wheelchair to enter and leave the space, and all controls, including locks and dispensers, must be accessible for wheelchair-bound passengers.

Onboard wheelchairs must have removable foot and armrests, safety belts, and backrests and wheel locks to allow airline personnel to assist passengers in transfers. The onboard wheelchair must be able to be easily pushed, pulled and turned on the cabin floor space.

Services and Equipment

Airlines must provide ground, boarding and onboard wheelchairs, as well as ramps or other mechanical devices used to assist in boarding and deplaning. Airline personnel are obliged to assist passengers store and retrieve carry-on luggage, move to and from seats, prepare for eating, use an onboard wheelchair, and move to and from the lavatory.

Airlines are responsible for transferring disabled passengers on interline flights between gates, and unless passengers are accompanied by an attendant, must not be left unattended for a period of more than 30 minutes.

Airlines are not permitted to charge passengers for providing facilities, equipment, and/or services, except for supplying oxygen canisters.

Passengers are required to provide at least 48-hour advance notice and one-hour advance check-in for the following:

- accommodations for 10 or more disabled passengers who travel as a group
- carriage of an electric wheelchair on an airplane with fewer than 60 seats

- connection of a respirator
- onboard wheelchair
- oxygen supply
- carriage by stretcher

Complaints and Legal Recourse

Each airline must make available a Complaints Resolution Officer (CRO) at each airport. Although this person is empowered to act on behalf of the airlines, his/her decision can be overruled by the pilot-in-command for safety reasons. Each airline must also have available a copy of the Air Carrier Access Act regulations. Passengers are entitled to request the regulation and refer to it as necessary. If a satisfactory resolution is not reached, the CRO shall provide a written statement setting forth the facts and reasons for the decision and inform the passenger of the right to pursue enforcement action by the Department of Transportation.

A formal written complaint to the airline should include all information pertaining to the circumstances of the alleged discrimination. In addition, the passenger should state whether a CRO was contacted, the name of the CRO, and date of contact and include any written response from the CRO.

Source: *U.S. Department of Transportation*

ICAO - ACCESS TO AIR TRANSPORT BY PERSONS WITH DISABILITIES

In 1999, the International Civil Aviation Organization (ICAO, see Appendix 6) issued Circular 274, entitled *Access to Air Transport by Persons with Disabilities*. This contains guidance material concerning access to air services and airport facilities by elderly and disabled persons which updates the Standards and Recommended Practices (SARPs) that were developed from the original guidance material. The original SARPs were introduced by the Tenth Session of the Facilitation Division into ICAO Annex 9 in 1988, and new SARPs were introduced at the Eleventh Session of the Facilitation Division in 1995 to address all aspects of air transport accessibility by a *person with reduced mobility*. The most important SARPs are listed below under the categories of *General*, *Access to Airports*, and *Access to Air Services*.

General

Persons with disabilities, when traveling, should be provided with special assistance in order to ensure that they receive services customarily available to the general public.

ICAO Contracting States should take necessary measures to make accessible to persons with disabilities all elements of a journey.

ICAO Contracting States should take necessary measures for the establishment of minimum uniform standards of accessibility, with respect to transportation services for persons with disabilities, by airlines, airports, and ground handling operators.

ICAO Contracting States should take necessary measures with airlines, airports, ground handling operators, and travel agents to ensure that persons with disabilities are provided information required; and that airlines, airports, ground handling operators, and travel agents are in a position to provide persons with disabilities with the assistance necessary for them.

ICAO Contracting States should take necessary measures to ensure the cooperation of airlines, airports, and ground handling operators to establish and coordinate training programs for personnel to assist persons with disabilities.

Access to Airports

ICAO Contracting States should ensure that lifting devices are available to facilitate the movement of elderly and disabled passengers between the airplane and the terminal building at arrival and departure points.

Measures should be taken to ensure that hearing- and vision-impaired passengers are able to obtain flight information.

Reserved points should be located as close as possible to the main entrances of airports for elderly or disabled persons being set down or picked up at a terminal building.

Parking facilities should be provided for persons with mobility needs, and measures should be taken to facilitate their movement between parking areas and the terminal buildings.

Access to Air Services

ICAO Contracting States should introduce provisions by which new airplanes and airplanes receiving major overhauls should conform to minimum uniform standards of accessibility with regard to onboard equipment, including movable armrests, onboard wheelchairs, lavatories, proper lighting and signage.

Wheelchairs, and other equipment, required by persons with disabilities, should be carried free of charge in the cabin, where safety and space requirements permit, or should be designated as priority baggage. Service animals accompanying persons with disabilities should also be carried free of charge in the cabin, subject to any national or airline regulations.

Persons with disabilities should be able to determine whether or not they need an escort to travel without the requirement of a medical certificate. Airlines can only demand medical clearance if the safety or well being of that passenger or other passengers cannot be guaranteed.

Source: *ICAO*

IATA - ACCEPTANCE AND CARRIAGE OF INCAPACITATED PASSENGERS

In the 1970s, the International Air Transport Association (IATA, see Appendix 6) developed and issued *Resolution 700* and *Recommended Practice 1700*, detailing the rules governing the acceptance and carriage of incapacitated passengers by IATA Member airlines. The only difference is that *Recommended Practice 1700* applies to Canada and the United States, whereas *Resolution 700* covers the rest of the world. The most important provisions of *Resolution 700* and *Recommended Practice 1700* are listed below.

Acceptance

IATA Member airlines agree to *interline transactions* concerning the carriage of incapacitated passengers, except:

- when their physical or medical condition could pose a threat to the safety of the other passengers, crew or airplane
- their condition renders them unable to assist in the evacuation of the airplane

Medical Clearance

Airlines cannot request medical clearance or special forms from incapacitated and senior passengers who require assistance in the airport or when boarding or deplaning. The airlines may request medical clearance by a qualified physician if the airline obtains information that passengers:

- suffer from a disease that is believed to be communicable or actively contagious

- may be a potential hazard to the safety of the flight

- might require medical attention and/or special medical equipment to maintain their health during the flight

Medical Forms

MEDIF—A Medical Information Form *must be completed and submitted by passengers:*

- whose fitness to travel is questionable based on recent instability, disease, treatment or operation

- whose medical condition dictates that special equipment be used in flight; for example, a stretcher, oxygen or a respirator

FREMEC—A *Frequent Traveler's Medical Card* is issued to facilitate air travel by regular and frequent passengers who are permanently or chronically incapacitated.

Ticketing

Incapacitated passengers' escorts shall always be ticketed separately.

Ground and In-Flight Handling Equipment

When wheelchairs, oxygen, stretchers, lifting services, devices for supporting limbs, and any other specialized equipment to support incapacitated passengers is provided by an IATA Member airline or its handling agent, the equipment or service will be provided in accordance with an IATA Member airline's policies, government regulations, and applicable rates and charges based on the Member airline's tariffs and regulations.

Procedures

At check-in, it should be verified that all provisions required for the assistance and carriage of incapacitated passengers have been made available. If it is discovered at check-in that an incapacitated passenger has not met requirements expected of them, the airline will endeavor to make arrangements to fulfill them without delaying the flight.

If time and circumstances do not permit this to be done, incapacitated passengers may travel if they and the IATA Member airline agrees that the passenger is able to adequately care for themself during the flight.

Refusal or Removal of Passengers

If an IATA Member airline denies transportation to incapacitated passengers at a point of origin or connecting point, the Member airline is responsible for immediately notifying all downline transfer stations and the destination station shown on the passenger's ticket, stating the reason for refusal/removal and full details of any action taken.

Availability of Wheelchairs and Other Equipment

IATA Member airlines shall endeavor to make available wheelchairs for boarding and deplaning, and within all airport facilities at departure, any midpoints and arrival. Airlines shall endeavor not to restrict the movement of incapacitated passengers within the airport.

Passengers may ask to have their own folding wheelchairs, or other equipment, carried in the passenger cabin where storage facilities are available. These requests are to be dealt with on a first come first served basis. If said facilities do not exist, wheelchairs or other equipment are to be stored as baggage.

Passengers who intend to check in their own wheelchair have the choice of using a wheelchair provided by the airline within the airport, or using their own wheelchair within the airport, and be permitted to use it until they reach the airplane door.

IATA Member airlines shall endeavor to have an onboard wheelchair capable of carrying incapacitated passengers to enable them to use the lavatory. Furthermore, IATA Member airlines shall endeavor to make available for passengers stretchers, blankets, pillows, nursing materials, and privacy curtains.

Boarding and Seating Passengers

Incapacitated passengers and their escorts shall normally be offered preboarding facilities.

Incapacitated passengers shall not normally be restricted from seats or seating areas, except when government or Member airline regulations concerning seating and safety are observed.

Loading of Equipment

Equipment required by incapacitated passengers not carried in the passenger cabin, shall be loaded in the baggage hold, and made easily accessible for timely return to the passenger. All items must be properly identified and tagged.

Staff Responsibilities

When interline connections are involved, the delivering Member airline will have completed its responsibility when the passenger is transferred to and accepted by the receiving Member airline.

In the event of schedule irregularities, causing the passenger to miss the connection with the receiving Member airline, or a cancellation of a flight by the receiving Member airline, it shall be the responsibility of the delivering Member airline to make whatever arrangements are necessary for the care and welfare of the passenger.

Source: *IATA*

IATA PASSENGER CONDITIONS OF CONTRACT & CARRIAGE

The first standard format of an international passenger ticket, and the procedures to be used for its completion, together with a set of general transport conditions applicable to both passengers and baggage, were adopted by the International Air Traffic Association (IATA) at its 17th General Meeting, held in Vienna, 18-19 February 1927. This had been the result of more than two years of detailed discussions and compromise between traffic and legal experts to develop a standard ticket, since the conditions of contract shown on an airline ticket must not only be acceptable to the airlines themselves but must also be in conformity with the laws of a large number of countries with different legal codes.

The conditions of contract contain notices advising passengers, among other things, that liability may be limited by the Warsaw Convention and related Protocols dealing with that Convention. Over the years, continuous and detailed consideration has been given to improve and refine the conditions of contract and carriage through the IATA Traffic Conference machinery, as reflected in a set of IATA Resolutions and Recommended Practices (RPs). The conditions of contract are mandatory for IATA Member airlines by virtue of IATA Resolutions 724 — *Notice and Conditions of Contract.*

The conditions of carriage must, of course, include many other points not specifically covered by the conditions of contract. In essence, the conditions of carriage represent the more detailed rules governing the relationship between the carriers and their customers. On the passenger side, they deal with such diverse topics as: changes to schedules; cancellation of flights; reservations; refunds; items unacceptable as baggage; and the conditions under which animals may be carried on board.

The General Conditions of Carriage for Passengers and Baggage pertaining to international air transportation are contained in IATA Recommended Practice 1724. The text of this Recommended Practice is being used by many international airlines as written, or with some specific amendments. These conditions of carriage are an integral part of the international airline ticket.

Medical Forms & Questionnaires

Depending on their medical condition and airline of choice, passengers may be required to fill-in medical forms or answer questionnaires so that their airlines will be able to establish accurate personal medical profiles prior to the passengers' journeys. In many cases, airlines use these questionnaires to create permanent electronic records within their computer reservation systems (CRSs) in order to allow their booking agents to adapt the airline's service capabilities to best meet the requirements of these special needs passengers.

The following is an overview of information categories and question types that special needs passengers are likely to encounter, whether on actual medical forms or during interview sessions with airline personnel. Many of these questions can be answered by passengers alone, but some will require the input of their physician. It should be noted that the best way for a passenger to prepare for a form/interview of this kind is simply to have all their personal medical details clearly listed and readily available before they begin the booking process.

Preliminary Information

- Passenger's name and contact information
- The name and contact information of the passenger's physician(s)
- Basic travel itinerary

Special Arrangements

- Does the passenger require special seating?

- Does the passenger require special meals?

- Does the passenger require a wheelchair?
  (if yes, then what category: WCHC?; WCHR?; WCHS?; etc. see acronyms in Appendix 3)

- Does the passenger require a stretcher?

- Will the passenger be travelling with an attendant or travel companion?
  (if yes, then name, sex, contact details, professional qualifications, etc.)

- Does the passenger need oxygen equipment in flight?

- Does the passenger require the use of any other special apparatus?

- Does the passenger require hospitalization?

- Do the passenger's needs require different attention on the ground than they do in the air?

- Will the passenger require special assistance at any connecting points in their itinerary? Upon arrival at their destination?

Medical Information
(may require physician's assistance)

- Diagnosis in detail (including vital signs)

- Dates of first symptoms, and of any operations or treatments that followed

- Prognosis for the flight

- Is the passenger's condition contagious or communicable?

(continued)

- Does the passenger require any medication other than that which will be self-administered?
- Could the passenger's condition cause stress or discomfort to other passengers?
- Can the passenger use a normal aircraft seat when it's in the UPRIGHT position?
- Can the passenger see to their own on-board needs and airport needs unassisted?

Directory of Companies and Organizations referred to in the *Air Travel Guide*

This appendix includes the various organizations and companies mentioned in the different sections and *Helpful Hints* of the *Air Travel Guide.*

Those organizations offering specific services to seniors and disabled travelers are listed in order of their appearance in the *Guide.* These listings are followed by one containing the world's major civil and commercial aviation organizations, mentioned in various parts of the book and described in Appendix 6 .

Finally, several additional organizations, not mentioned in this *Guide* but notable nonetheless for their website resources relating to travel and medical issues, have also been included at the end of this appendix.

Companies and Organizations offering Specific Services

The Oxygen Traveler
(oxygen supplies delivered while abroad)
tel: (937) 433-6007

Travel Aides International
(personal assistants)
tel: (530) 872-2479

Wheelers Inc.
(wheelchair and scooter-accessible vans in US)
tel: (800) 456-1371

Wheelchair Getaways
(wheelchair and scooter-accessible vans in US)
tel: (800) 642-2042

Convaid
(lightweight stroller manufacturers)
tel: (888) 266-8243

International Association for Medical Assistance to Travelers
(lists of English-speaking physicians around the world, and other services)
tel: (716) 754-4883

Major International Aviation Organizations

International Civil Aviation Organization (ICAO)
(UN civil aviation body)
tel: (514) 954-8219
www.icao.int

International Air Transport Association (IATA)
(association representing the world's major airlines)
tel: (514) 874-0202
www.iata.org

Airports Council International (ACI)
(association representing the world's major airports)
tel: (41) 22 717-8585
www.airports.org

Additional Useful Organizations

Highway to Health
(detailed health-services information for cities all over the world)
www.hthworldwide.com

International Society of Travel Medicine
(list of travel clinics worldwide, by city, including breakdown of services available at each)
www.istm.org

International SOS
(agency providing 24-hour medical resource assistance on 5 continents)
www.internationalsos.com

Lonely Planet - Health
(good advice for people taking excursions off the beaten-path)
www.lonelyplanet.com/health

MASTA Online
(immunizations, prescriptions, and other useful advice)
www.masta.org

Society for Accessible Travel and Hospitality (SATH)
(well-researched and presented resources for the disabled traveler, including a very good newsletter)
www.who.int/ith/english/index.htm

World Health Organization
(vaccination requirements and travel advice)
www.who.int/ith/english

Abbreviations and Acronyms

A/P	Airplane *or* Airport
ABP	Able-bodied passenger
ACI	Airports Council International
AED	Automatic external defibrillator
ARS	Airline reservation system
ATB	Automated ticket/boarding pass
BLND	Blind passenger
CAA	Civil aviation authority
CBBG	Cabin baggage
CM	Crew member
CRO	Complaints resolution officer
CRS	Computer reservation system
CUST	Customs
DBC	Denied boarding compensation
DBML	Diabetic meal
DEAF	Deaf passenger
DG	Dangerous goods
EPTV	Elevating passenger transfer vehicle
ET	Electronic ticketing
FA	Flight attendant
FAA	Federal Aviation Administration (USA)
FREMEC	Frequent traveler's medical card
GFML	Gluten free meal
GH	Ground handling
HFML	High fiber meal
IATA	International Air Transport Association
ICAO	International Civil Aviation Organization
LCML	Low calorie meal
LEGB	Legs in cast—both

LEGL	Leg in cast—left
LEGR	Leg in cast—right
LFML	Low fat/low cholesterol meal
LPML	Low protein meal
LSML	Low sodium meal
MAAS	Meet and assist
MEDA	Medical case
MEDIF	Medical information form
NLML	Non-lactose meal
OXYG	Oxygen required
PAL	Passenger access lift
PB	Passenger bridge
PIC	Pilot-in-command
PSM	Passenger service message
PTV	Passenger transport vehicle
Res.	Resolution (IATA)
RP	Recommended Practice (IATA)
TDD	Telephone device for the deaf
TKT	Ticket
TT	Tele-typewriter
SPML	Special meal and type
STCR	Stretcher passenger
WCBD	Wheelchair dry cell battery
WCBW	Wheelchair wet cell battery
WCHC	Wheelchair for cabin seat
WCHR	Wheelchair for ramp
WCHS	Wheelchair for steps
WCMP	Wheelchair manual powered
WCOB	Wheelchair onboard requested

Pictogram glossary

Information

First Aid

Exit

No Entry

Fire Extinguisher

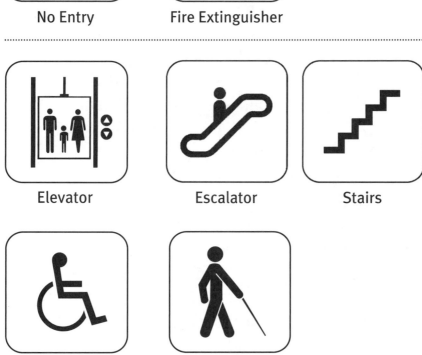

Elevator

Escalator

Stairs

Wheelchair

Access to Persons
with Reduced Mobility

Taxis

Taxis and Buses

Bus Transport

Car Rental

Boat or Ferry

Trains

Helicopter

Accommodation
Information

Parking

Baggage Claim

Baggage Locker

Baggage Trolley

No Parking

No Smoking

No Dogs

No Firearms

Check-in Counter

Customs/
Passport

Customs/
Bag Check

Washrooms
Men and women

Washrooms
Men only

Washrooms
Women only

Shopping Area

Waiting Area

Barber

Restaurants

Bar

Coffee Shop

Currency
Exchange

Lost and Found

Coat Check

Pharmacy

Nursery

Water Fountain

Telephone

Volume-Adjustable
Telephone

Keypad
Telephone

Cable Telegram

Post Office

Braille Services

Services Available for
the Hearing-Impaired

Signing Services
Available

Audio Description
Available

Audiovisual
Description
Available

Technical Design Recommendations for Airports

Airports Council International (ACI) has been active in promoting and legislating change within its Member airports to improve facilities and services for seniors and disabled persons. The ACI publication *Airports and Persons with Disabilities* contains some technical design recommendations for airports, including the following.

Doors

Timed doors should remain open for a minimum of 5 seconds. Alternatively, automatic hinged doors work well, as long as there is a space of between 120-150 cm. (50-60 in.) on the opening side of the door. For the aforementioned door, lever handles are preferable to knob handles, and should be not more than 85 cm. (33 in.) above floor level. All doors should have a width no less than 95 cm. (37 in.) and the floor on either side of the door should be flat. Glass doors should always be clearly marked with a bright yellow strip sticker. Glass doors are sometimes difficult to detect, and individuals, particularly sight-impaired passengers, are known to walk into them. All doors designed for use by disabled passengers should be marked with the international wheelchair symbol.

Stairways

In order to make a stairway safe and manageable, steps should have a maximum height of 14-16 cm. (5.5-6 in.), a minimum depth of 28-32 cm. (11-12.5 in.), and a minimum width of 150 cm. (60 in.).

To aid the sight-impaired, the first and last step of a stairway should be marked with a contrasting color or surface texture. A strip of different contrasting color should be used on all other steps.

A set of steps should not exceed 170 cm. (67 in.) in height, or 12 steps. Any number beyond this makes it too difficult to proceed. A stairway that extends beyond 12 steps should include a landing (after 12 steps), whose length is equivalent to the width of the stairway. Preferably, the landing should be able to serve as a rest area, complete with a bench.

Handrails, at a height of 85-90 cm. (33.5-34 in.) from the step, should be provided on both sides of the stairway. Wide stairways should have a central handrail added, and all handrails should be rounded. Handrails should extend at least 30 cm. (12 in.) beyond the bottom and top step, and should be continuous throughout stair runs and landing areas.

Raised tread strips at the sides of steps and landings will aid cane and stick users.

Moving Walkways and Ramps

The gradient of the moving walkway should not exceed 8 percent. If a walkway gradient does exceed 8 percent, it should be indicated by a sign.

A ramp should not have a gradient of more than 6 percent, and one that extends more than 6 meters (20 ft.) should be broken with a horizontal intermediate landing of no less than 1.5 meters (5 ft.) square. As is the case with a moving walkway, a sign indicating that a ramp gradient exceeds 6 percent should be posted.

The width of a ramp should be at least 200 cm. (80 in.), with handrails 85 cm. (33.5 in.) in height on either side. A temporary ramp, without handrails, should have 5 cm. (2 in.) high curbs to prevent wheelchair wheels from rolling off the edge.

Elevators

The maneuvering area in front of the elevator door should be no less than 150 X 150 cm. (60 in.). The floor of the maneuvering area, and the floor of the elevator itself, should have slip-resistant tiles.

The elevator should have a width of at least 110 cm. (43 in.) and a depth of at least 140 cm. (55 in.), with a doorway width of at least 90 cm. (35 in.). The doorway should have horizontal light beams, located at 20 cm. and 60 cm. (8 and 23 in.) in height, which prevent the door from closing if wheelchair or senior passengers have not entered or exited the elevator.

Operating panels inside and outside the elevator should be no higher than 85 cm. (33.5 in.) above floor level, and a handrail should hug all walls just below the level of the operating panel.

Waiting Areas and Concession Stands

The height of counters or vending machine collection points and coin slots should not exceed 75 cm. (30 in.) and aisles in stores and restaurants should measure at least 90 cm. (35 in.).

Telephones

The door of a closed cabin telephone should be easy to open and close, with a handle at a level of 85 cm. (33.5 in.), and a retractable seat should be used to allow wheelchair entry.

Directories should be within easy reach, operating instructions should be worded clearly, and if possible, the letters raised. The bottom of the telephone unit should not exceed the height of 80 cm. (31.5 in.).

Toilets

- The clearance of toilet doors must be at least 90 cm. (35 in.).
- Toilet doors must open outward.
- Level of the door handle should be 85 cm. (33.5 in.).
- A crossbar should be mounted on the inner side of the swing door at the same level as the door handle.
- Light switch should be 85 cm. (33.5 in.) above the floor.
- Floor tiles should be of nonskid material.
- The height of toilet seat should be 48 cm. (19 in.).
- There should be at least 95 cm. (37 in.) of space on either side of the toilet to allow wheelchair access.
- Support railings, able to tolerate a weight of 150 kg. (330 lbs.), should be present on either side of the toilet.
- Toilet paper should be within easy reach.
- A handle for flushing should be within easy reach.
- Washstand should not be smaller than 55 cm. (22 in.) and mounted at a height between 82 and 85 cm. (32 and 33.5 in.).
- Soap and paper towel dispensers should be in the vicinity of the washstand and within easy reach.
- Emergency call switch should be installed at a height of 85 cm. (33.5 in.). A second emergency switch, in the form of a pull chain, should be installed at a maximum height of 15 cm. (6 in.) for one who falls to the floor.
- Location of toilets for the disabled should be clearly indicated with the international wheelchair symbol.

Major International Aviation Organizations

INTERNATIONAL CIVIL AVIATION ORGANIZATION (ICAO)

Headquartered in Montreal, Canada, ICAO is a specialized agency of the United Nations, which provides the machinery for the achievement of international cooperation in the air. The Organization was established after the Chicago Convention on International Civil Aviation of 1944 addressed the importance of developing a basic legal framework for the operation of international civil air services. It represents 186 Member States.

ICAO is made up of an *Assembly*, a *Council*, and a *Secretariat*, whose activities focus on seven major categories:

- standardization
- communications, navigation, surveillance/air traffic management (CNS/ATM)
- facilitation
- economics
- technical co-operation for development
- international air law

Facilitation of International Air Transport

From the beginning of ICAO's history, the need for facilitation of international air transport—the removal of obstacles in order to promote the free, expeditious and unimpeded passage of an aircraft, its passengers, crew, baggage, cargo and mail across international boundaries—was evident. This need is inherent in the speed of air travel itself; if, for example, customs, immigration, public health and other formalities require one hour at each end of a transoceanic flight of six hours, the total duration of the trip is increased by more than 30 percent. Similarly, the cost of aircraft has made it imperative to minimize unproductive time spent on the ground. New requirements for the security of air transport and for eradicating illegal traffic in narcotics have imposed additional forms of border control, thus increasing the challenge for the facilitation program to find new ways of expediting aircraft and their loads rapidly and efficiently.

ICAO has therefore developed a comprehensive facilitation program over the years which is reflected in the International Standards and Recommended Practices (SARPs) of Annex 9 to the Chicago Convention, pertinent Resolutions of the Assembly, as well as recommendations and statements of the Council and the Facilitation Division. Broadly speaking, the facilitation program aims at:

- eliminating all unessential documentary requirements
- simplifying and standardizing the remaining forms
- providing minimum facilities at airports
- simplifying handling and clearance procedures

In addition to reducing documentary and procedural formalities, ICAO's efforts in the facilitation field are aimed at the provision of adequate airport terminal buildings for passengers and their baggage, as well as for air cargo, with all related facilities and services. Special attention is given to improving the accessibility of air transport for elderly and disabled passengers. With the rapid growth of air transport, it is necessary for airport administrations to review the adequacy of their facilities at regular intervals.

INTERNATIONAL AIR TRANSPORT ASSOCIATION (IATA)

IATA, the trade association of the international airline industry, was originally founded in 1919. Today it represents more than 95 percent of all international scheduled air traffic. IATA is headquartered in Montreal, Canada; has its executive office in Geneva, Switzerland; and regional offices in Amman, Jordan; Beijing, China; Brussels, Belgium; Dakar, Senegal; London, United Kingdom; Miami, United States, Nairobi, Kenya; Santiago, Chile; Singapore; and Washington, DC, United States. In addition, there are currently more than 90 offices around the world.

IATA Board of Governors

The Board of Governors is composed of 31 representatives from Member airlines, which acts on behalf and in the interest of the association, and which reports to the IATA Annual General Meeting. It gives policy directives and guidance to IATA standing committees and to subsidiary bodies and act in close cooperation and coordination with the Director General and Chief Executive Officer.

IATA's Principal Objectives

- promote safe, reliable and secure air services
- achieve recognition of the importance of a healthy air transport industry to worldwide social and economic development
- assist the industry to achieve adequate levels of profitability

- provide high quality, value for money, industry-required products and services that meet the needs of the customer
- develop cost-effective, environmentally-friendly standards and procedures to facilitate the operation of international air transport
- identify and articulate common industry positions and support the resolution of key industry issues

Facilitation of International Air Transport

The basic aim of the IATA facilitation activities is to improve the procedures and facilities used for the clearance of aircraft, crew, passengers, baggage and cargo, both inbound and outbound. This requires industry efforts throughout the year to standardize, simplify, or eliminate government formalities relating to international travel and trade, in close cooperation with the International Civil Aviation Organization (ICAO), Airports Council International (ACI), World Customs Organization (WCO), World Tourism Organization (WTO), World Travel & Tourism Council (WTTC), and many other international, regional, and national organizations involved in the development of international tourism and trade. In this context, it should be noted that IATA has developed industry standards for carrying disabled passengers, as reflected in IATA Resolution 700 and IATA Recommended Practice 1700.

AIRPORTS COUNCIL INTERNATIONAL (ACI)

Airports Council International (ACI) was established in 1991 to represent the world's airports, and currently has 530 Members operating over 1,400 airports in 162 countries and territories. The nonprofit organization's prime purpose is to foster cooperation among its Member airports and with other partners in world aviation, including governments, airlines, and aircraft manufacturing organizations. Through this cooperation, ACI makes a significant contribution to providing the traveling public with an air transport system that is safe, secure, efficient and environmentally compatible.

ACI is headquartered in Geneva, Switzerland, with regional offices in Brussels, Belgium for Europe; Cairo, Egypt for Africa; Caracas, Venezuela for Latin America/Caribbean; New Delhi, India for Asia; Vancouver, Canada for the Pacific; and Washington, DC, United States for North America. ACI also has a liaison office with ICAO in Montreal, Canada.

ACI's Principal Objectives

- promote legislation, regulations and international agreements that support Member airports' interests
- contribute to increased cooperation, mutual assistance, information exchange and learning opportunities for Member airports
- provide Member airports with timely information and analysis of domestic and international developments
- develop and promote programs that stimulate public awareness of the economic and social importance of airports.

- generate programs and services which meet members' needs and contribute to membership retention and growth

ACI World Governing Board

The World Governing Board, composed of 29 representatives from Member airports, meets at least twice annually. An Executive Committee, consisting of eight members, meets more frequently to supervise the implementation of Board decisions.

The ACI World Standing Committees, consisting of experts from all regions, are responsible for research. They also recommend policies in five areas of broad concern to airport operators: economics; environment; facilitation; security; and technical/safety.

ACI's supreme authority rests with the General Assembly, which consists of all regular Members and meets once annually.

Facilitation of International Air Transport

An important ACI activity is in the field of facilitation. This covers passengers; baggage; freight and mail; automated services; surface access to airports; dangerous goods; measures to combat drug trafficking; and the relationship between facilitation and security. An essential part of this activity is the development of recommendations intended to assist airports meet the needs of persons with disabilities when improving existing facilities and designing new ones.

Glossary

able-bodied passenger See *passenger, able-bodied (ABP)*.

agent, authorized A responsible person who represents an operator and who is authorized by or on behalf of such operator to act on all formalities connected with the entry and clearance of the operator's aircraft, crew, passengers, cargo, mail, baggage or stores (ICAO Annex 9).

agent, passenger See *check-in agent* and *gate agent*.

agent, passenger sales See *passenger sales agency*.

agent, ticket See *ticket agent*.

air cargo
1) Anything carried or to be carried in an aircraft, except mail, or baggage carried under a passenger ticket and baggage check, but includes baggage moving under an air waybill or shipment record (IATA RP 1601— *Conditions of Carriage for Cargo*).
2) Any property carried or to be carried in an aircraft, other than mail or other property carried under the terms of an international postal convention, baggage or property of the carrier, provided that baggage moving under an air waybill is cargo (IATA RP 1608).
3) Any property carried on an aircraft other than mail, stores and accompanied or mishandled baggage (ICAO Annex 9).

air law At the national level, most states have enacted national aviation acts or codes covering a wide range of civil aviation matters, such as airworthiness of aircraft; aircraft registration; aircraft safety; aircraft noise certification; licensing of flight crews, aircraft maintenance personnel and air traffic controllers; aircraft flight operation; airport services; aircraft and airport security and safety; and the transport of *dangerous goods* by air.

airbridge A mechanically operated, adjustable ramp to provide direct access between aircraft and airport terminal. Synonymous with *Jetway* and *loading bridge*.

aircraft cabin The passenger compartment of an aircraft, excluding cockpit/flight deck, that is usually divided into zones for the purpose of seat classification (first class, business class and economy class). In combi-aircraft, a section of the main cabin is used for cargo.

aircraft emergency equipment Those items of equipment carried on an aircraft for use in emergency procedures, such as first aid kits, oxygen equipment, defibrillators, fire extinguishers, incubators, stretchers, evacuation equipment, life rafts and jackets, landing and signal flares, emergency locator transmitters and underwater locator devices.

aircraft ground handling The processing of passengers, baggage, cargo and mail, including aircraft crew, by an airline or its appointed handling agent at an airport.

aircraft security See *security, aviation*.

airline A legal entity, such as an association, company, corporation, organization or partnership, holding an operating certificate issued by the *civil aviation authority* of the state of registry, to engage in the business of providing scheduled and/or nonscheduled air transport services for the carriage of passengers, baggage, and/or cargo and/or mail. Synonymous with *air carrier, carrier* and *operator*.

airline agent Any person who has authority, express or implied, to act for or on behalf of a carrier in relation to the carriage of passengers, baggage, cargo or mail. See also *agent, authorized*.

airline, booking The airline with which the passenger made his/her original reservations or with which additional reservations were made after commencement of the journey. Where a booking is made with, or through, or is handed over to a computer reservation system (CRS), the host airline's CRS will be considered as the *booking airline* (IATA Res. 766).

airline, connecting The airline to whose services the passenger and his/her baggage or the cargo are to be transferred for onward connecting transportation (IATA RP 1008, 1608).

airline, first The participating airline over whose air routes the first section of carriage under the air waybill or ticket and baggage check is undertaken or performed (IATA RP 1008, 1608). Synonymous with *originating airline*.

airline, forwarding The airline responsible for the condition which creates a need for involuntary change in the passenger's journey; on missed connections the airline on whose flight a passenger is originally ticketed to be carried to a connection point is the forwarding airline (IATA RP 1008).

airline reservation system (ARS) An on-line application in which a computing system is used to keep track of seat inventories, flight schedules and other related information required to run an airline. The reservation system is designed to maintain up-to-date data files and to respond within seconds or less to inquiries from ticket agents at locations remote from the computing system.

airline, ticketing An airline whose automated tickets are issued through the computer system of a servicing airline by imprinting the ticketing airline's name and numeric code (IATA RP 1008).

airline, transferring The participating airline transferring passengers, baggage, cargo or mail to a receiving airline at a transfer point (synonymous with interline point) for onward transportation.

airport (A/P) A defined area on land or water (including any buildings, installations and equipment) intended to be used either wholly or in part for the arrival, departure and surface movement of aircraft.

There are approximately 15,500 airports worldwide, including more than 300 water airports and 750 heliports for public use. 6,000 airports are served by both *scheduled* domestic and international flights. According to data published by ICAO, approximately 1,050 regular and alternate airports serve *international* scheduled, and/or nonscheduled, and/or general aviation operations.

airport terminal A generic term indicating the buildings and facilities used for the handling of aircraft, passengers, baggage, cargo and mail.

ambulatory passenger See *disabled passenger.*

automated ticket/boarding pass (ATB) The form of an automated ticket and boarding pass described in IATA RP 1722c. It is a single copy noncarbonized ticket (normally on card stock) with each coupon imprinted separately. Each coupon used for air transport is comprised of a flight coupon and a detachable passenger coupon and boarding pass for a specific flight. One coupon is issued as the passenger receipt which together with all passenger coupons and boarding passes builds up the passenger copy of the passenger ticket and baggage check (IATA RP 1008).

aviation security See *security, aviation.*

baggage Articles, effects and other personal property of a passenger as are necessary or appropriate for wear, use, comfort or convenience in connection with his/her trip. Unless otherwise specified, it includes both checked and unchecked baggage of the passenger (IATA RP 1008 and 1724).

baggage allowance, free The baggage which may be carried without payment of a charge in addition to the fare (IATA RP 1008). The free baggage allowance is determined by each airline as part of their tariff. This allowance includes checked baggage (i.e., baggage carried in the aircraft hold) and unchecked baggage (or carry-on baggage), i.e., baggage that remains in the custody of the passenger in the aircraft cabin.

In general, the free baggage allowance is expressed in one of the following two ways:

- *weight concept* defines the amount of baggage entitled by the passenger's ticket in kilograms. For example, an economy-class passenger may be entitled to 20 kg (44 lb) of baggage, a business-class passenger to 30 kg (66 lb) and a first-class passenger to 40 kg. (88 lb)

- *piece concept* defines the amount of baggage entitled by the passenger's ticket by the number of bags. Generally, the *piece concept* allows two pieces of checked baggage for each passenger, each piece weighing not more than 32 kg (70 lb) and measuring not more than 158 cm (62 in) adding the dimensions: height + width + length

The *piece concept* is generally in use on flights within, to and from Canada and the United States whereas the *weight concept* is generally used in the rest of the world. Under both systems, the total free baggage allowance includes checked plus unchecked baggage together. Also under both systems, the free baggage allowance is generally defined as those items necessary for the passenger's journey, such as clothing and personal articles within certain limitations.

In general, disabled passengers are allowed a wheelchair in addition to their free baggage allowance, but it is usually processed as checked baggage.

baggage, cabin (CBBG) Baggage of which the passenger retains custody (IATA RP 1008). This covers personal belongings, such as briefcases, handbags and other nonbulky baggage conforming to specified dimensions, to permit stowage aboard the aircraft. For safety reasons, it is the responsibility of the carrier to ensure that all baggage carried onto an aircraft and taken into the passenger cabin has been screened by security agents and is adequately and securely stowed in overhead luggage bins or fitted underneath seats. Synonymous with *carry-on baggage*, *hand baggage* and *unchecked baggage*.

baggage, carry-on See *baggage, cabin*.

boarding check The final check of travel documents after which passengers are admitted to boarding lounge or *passenger transport vehicle (PTV)*.

boarding pass See *automated ticket/boarding pass*.

booking airline See *airline, booking*.

cabin baggage See *baggage, cabin*.

cabin crew duties The duties of aircraft cabin crew include the following:

- providing services and attending to passengers
- insuring that cabin baggage is properly stored in overhead luggage bins or safely fitted under seats
- insuring that passengers are made familiar with the location and use of seat belts, emergency exits, life jackets as appropriate, oxygen dispensing equipment and other emergency equipment provided for individual use

- competent execution of an in-flight and evacuation emergency, such as the use of portable fire extinguishers, oxygen equipment and first aid kits, life jackets, evacuation slides and life rafts

- awareness of the types of dangerous goods which may, and may not, be carried in a passenger cabin

carry-on baggage See *baggage, cabin.*

check-in agent A passenger agent assigned to check-in procedures for passengers and their baggage.

civil aviation authority (CAA) The authority of a state responsible for the establishment of all necessary provisions in its national laws or regulations for mandatory compliance by any civil aircraft registered in that state or operated by an operator who has his principal place of business or permanent address in that state. Synonymous with *civil aviation administration.*

complaints resolution officer (CRO) A representative of an airline that serves to resolve passengers' complaints. Only a pilot-in-command can overrule a CRO's decision because of safety reasons.

computer reservation system (CRS) In general terms, a computer system that provides information about airline schedules, space availability, tariffs and applicable conditions of sale, and through which reservations on air transport services can be made. In practice, most computer reservation systems (CRSs) also provide additional travel information and related services, including the issuance of tickets. Some or all of these facilities can be made available to other airlines and travel agents. With the impetus of deregulation, a very large proportion of passenger tickets are now being sold by travel agents; in some countries this has reached up to 90 percent of the total market. Concurrently, an increasing number of travel agents decided to subscribe to a computer reservation system (CRS) so as to take advantage of the large productivity gains offered by the use of a CRS and to improve services to customers. Today, commercial public computer networks offer direct access to CRSs by the traveling public through the use of personal computers.

conditions of carriage and contract See *passenger conditions of carriage and contract.*

connecting airline See *airline, connecting.*

customs (CUST) A government authority designated to control the flow of goods to/from a country and to collect the applicable import and export duties, covering both passengers/baggage and cargo. This includes the establishment of the rules, regulations and procedures involved.

dangerous goods (DG) Articles or substances which are capable of posing significant risk to health, safety or property when transported by air (ICAO Annex 6, 18).

dangerous goods in passenger baggage For safety reasons, dangerous goods as defined in the IATA *Dangerous Goods Regulations* (DGR) such as those listed below, shall *not be carried in or as passenger checked or carry-on baggage:*

- briefcases and security type attaché cases with installed alarm devices; or incorporative lithium batteries and/or pyrotechnic material
- explosives, munitions, fireworks and flares
- gases (flammable, nonflammable, deeply refrigerated and poisonous), such as camping gas and aerosols
- flammable liquids, such as lighter fuels, paints and thinner
- flammable solids, such as matches and articles which are easily ignited; substances liable to spontaneous combustion; substances which on contact with water emit flammable gases
- oxidizing substances, such as bleaching powder and peroxides
- poisonous (toxic) and infectious substances
- radioactive materials
- corrosives, such as acids, alkalis, mercury which may be contained in thermometers, and wet-cell batteries
- other dangerous articles, such as magnetized materials, offensive or irritating materials. Limited quantities of medicines and toilet articles which are necessary or appropriate for the passenger during the journey, such as hairsprays, perfumes and medicines containing alcohol may be carried (IATA Res. 745)

The use of portable electronic devices on board commercial aircraft is prohibited because of the potential for interference with onboard navigational and communications systems, such as AM/FM radios, CB radios, CD players, cellular telephones, electronic video games, laptop computers, remote-controlled toys, televisions and video cameras.

denied boarding compensation (DBC) Passengers who are denied boarding on a scheduled flight are entitled to compensation. In order to qualify, such passengers must be in possession of a valid ticket with a confirmed reservation for the particular flight shown on that ticket. They must also have presented themselves for check-in within the stipulated time limits and be in possession of the necessary travel documents, according to the *General Conditions of Carriage*. In the event that all passengers booked cannot be accommodated, first priority is normally given to disabled passengers and unaccompanied children.

Before denying boarding to any passenger, the airline concerned, or its handling agent, may call for volunteers not to board such flights. Passengers who are denied boarding, voluntarily or otherwise, shall have the choice of:

- full refund of the cost of the unused portion of the ticket
- rerouting to the final destination of the ticket presented at check-in by the first available flight(s) or at a later date at the passenger's convenience
- additionally, upon being denied boarding, each passenger is entitled to receive an amount established by the airline concerned or established jointly by the airlines serving a given country, paid in cash or, if acceptable to the passenger, in travel vouchers or credit towards future travel

Any passenger who accepts the denied boarding compensation does so as full settlement of any and all claims against the airline.

disabled passenger A passenger whose physical, medical or mental condition requires individual attention, during ground handling, on enplaning and deplaning, during flight, and in an emergency evacuation which is not normally extended to other passengers. This includes:

- medically ill or temporarily disabled persons (ambulatory or nonambulatory) whose condition is considered as variable and who, therefore, require medical clearance prior to each air journey.

- permanently handicapped persons whose condition (physical or mental) is stable and who, therefore, can either obtain a permanent or semipermanent medical clearance or be totally exempt from such clearance and only require special handling.

- *ambulatory* means a passenger who can walk and board the aircraft unassisted, even if slowly or with a cane or on crutches.

- *nonambulatory* means a passenger unable to walk and board the aircraft unassisted (IATA Res. 700 and RP 1700).

electronic ticketing See ticketing, electronic.

elevating passenger transfer vehicle See *passenger transfer vehicle, elevating (EPTV)*.

first airline See *airline, first*.

forwarding airline See *airline, forwarding*.

free baggage allowance See *baggage allowance, free*.

frequent traveler's medical card (FREMEC) A medical card for incapacitated, disabled or handicapped passengers, now generally replaced by proprietary airline forms and computer reservations profiles.

gate agent A passenger agent assigned to controlling and directing passengers upon boarding, and assisting and directing passengers after deplaning.

ground handling (GH) The handling of passengers, baggage, cargo and mail at airports, in terminals and warehouses, and to and from the aircraft (ISO).

handicapped passenger See *disabled passenger.*

hand baggage See *baggage, cabin.*

incapacitated passenger See *disabled passenger.*

interline connecting time intervals At most airports throughout the world minimum interline connecting time intervals, commonly called *minimum connecting times* (MCTs), have been established by airlines serving those airports. The basic objective of agreed connecting time intervals is to protect both the delivering and receiving airline's interests and insure that the passenger and his/her baggage can rely on making connections within the time specified.

interline connection A change of airline by a passenger at any intermediate point in the itinerary.

interline point Any point between airport of departure and airport of destination, as shown on ticket or air waybill, at which passengers, baggage or cargo will change from the flight of one airline to the flight of another airline, whether a connection or passenger stopover at such point is involved. All airports through which a city or adjacent cities are served by an airline being considered as a single interline point. Synonymous with *transfer point*.

jetway See *airbridge*.

loading bridge See *airbridge*.

medical information form (MEDIF) A form to facilitate air travel for incapacitated, disabled or handicapped passengers. This form is now generally replaced by proprietary airline forms and computer reservations profiles.

non-ambulatory passenger See *disabled passenger*.

passenger, able-bodied (ABP) A passenger selected by crew members to assist in managing emergency situations if and as required. In a planned emergency, able bodied passengers will be briefed on their responsibilities if time permits.

passenger access lift (PAL) See *passenger transfer vehicle, elevating*.

passenger bridge (PB) A mechanically operated, adjustable ramp to provide direct access between aircraft and terminal building or ground transport vehicles. Synonymous with *passenger boarding bridge* (PBB), *passenger loading bridge (PLB)* and *walkway*.

passenger conditions of carriage and contract The first standard format of an international airline ticket and air consignment note, commonly called air waybill, and the procedures to be used for their completion, together with a set of general transport conditions applicable to both passengers and goods. For more detailed information, see *IATA Passenger Conditions of Carriage and Contract* in Chapter 6.

passenger, disabled See *disabled passenger*.

passenger loading bridge (PLB) See *airbridge*.

passenger sales agency A travel agency accredited by an IATA member airline to sell international air transportation in accordance with the IATA *Passenger Sales Agency Rules* (IATA Res. 800). According to the *General Conditions of Carriage for Passengers and Baggage* (IATA RP 1724), the term *authorized agent* means a passenger sales agent who has been appointed by a carrier to represent the carrier in the sale of air passenger transportation over the services of the carrier and, when authorized, over the services of other air carriers.

passenger sales agent system An automated system in a travel agent's office used and controlled by the agent to record reservations, carry out accounting functions, etc. The agent's system, known as a stand-alone system, is not connected to any airline system although an interface with a vendor's computer reservation system (CRS) is often provided. The term *vendor* means a commercial enterprise that develops and sells CRS services.

passenger service message (PSM) As soon as possible after completion of check-in of passengers, airlines shall send a *passenger service message* (PSM) to the station(s) concerned of any passengers carried on a flight who require assistance or special handling. The format is described in IATA RP 1715.

passenger transfer vehicle, elevating (EPTV) A specially designed transport vehicle, resembling a bus, used on the apron for the transfer of passengers and crew members between the airport terminal building and remote aircraft stands, which can be elevated to different heights. The passengers walk into the vehicle, also called *mobile lounge*, through the boarding gate; the *pod* body is then lowered into the chassis for rapid transfer to the aircraft, where the pod is raised up to dock with the aircraft door and passengers board the aircraft, or vice versa. Synonymous with *elevating passenger transport vehicle* and *elevating transport vehicle* (ETV).

passenger transport vehicle (PTV) See *passenger transfer vehicle, elevating*.

passenger, wheelchair A passenger requiring the use of a wheelchair during the journey. The use of wheelchairs can be categorized as follows:

- *wheelchair for cabin seat (WCHC)* Passenger is completely immobile and requires wheelchair for entire time spent in airport terminal, and transfer to the airplane. Passenger must be carried up and down steps and to and from cabin seat (IATA).

- *wheelchair for ramp (WCHR)* Passenger can ascend/descend steps and make his/her own way to and from the cabin seat, but requires a wheelchair for distance to and from airport terminal and airplane (IATA).

- *wheelchair for steps (WCHS)* Passenger cannot ascend/descend steps, but is able to make his/her own way to and from cabin seat; requires wheelchair for distance to and from airport terminal and airplane, but must be carried up and down steps (IATA).

person with disabilities Any person whose mobility is reduced due to a physical incapacity (sensory or locomotor), an intellectual deficiency, age, illness or any other cause of disability when using transport and whose situation needs special attention and the adaptation to the person's needs of the services made available to all passengers (ICAO).

person with reduced mobility A person with limited physical capacity.

reservation system, computer See *computer reservation system (CRS)*.

seat pitch The distance between the front edge of one seat in an aircraft and the front edge of the seat immediately in front when both are in an upright position (IATA RP 1008). First-class seats have a greater pitch than the ones in business class and, in turn, business class seats have a greater pitch than the ones in economy- /tourist-class.

security, aviation The implementation of effective security controls and procedures by governments, airport authorities and airlines to insure the safety of passengers, crew, ground personnel and the general public at airports and in flight.

security screening In *civil aviation*, the application of technical or other means which are intended to detect weapons, explosives or other dangerous devices which may be used to commit an act of unlawful interference (ICAO Annex 17). In other words, a process for the examination of passengers, baggage, cargo or mail at airports which may include the use of security devices and equipment, selective visual examination, selective opening and/or physical search where permitted by law or regulation.

telephone device for the deaf (TDD) Telephone designed to assist deaf and/or hearing-impaired persons to communicate using special features, including volume control, teletype pad, and visual display.

ticket (TKT) The document, formally called *passenger ticket and baggage check*, issued by or on behalf of a carrier which includes the conditions of contract and notices, and the flight and passenger coupons contained therein. The ticket serves as evidence of payment of airfare and constitutes the passenger's written evidence of the contract of carriage, and detailed information to ensure proper processing and handling. For passengers carried internationally, the standard IATA passenger ticket and baggage check is issued under the provisions of the Warsaw Convention. For additional information, see *passenger conditions of carriage and contract* in Chapter 6.

The standard IATA passenger ticket and baggage check contains the following details:

- entire travel itinerary, i.e., place of origin, en route places, if any, at which the passenger will change carrier, flight or class, or will make a stopover, and place of destination
- flight number, class of service and status of reservation (either confirmed, requested but not confirmed, or subject to space being available, whenever fare or rule prohibits making advance reservation for each)

- fare calculation of the total fare for the complete itinerary covered by the ticket or conjunction ticket(s) in the currency of the country of commencement of transportation, unless otherwise provided by applicable currency regulations, and any restrictions applicable to the fare paid
- amount of taxes and other charges paid
- applicable free baggage allowance in kilograms or pounds and number of checked pieces; a separate flight coupon is provided for each part of the journey between places of origin and destination entailing a change of carrier, flight or class, or a stopover

In addition to serving as evidence of contract between passenger and carrier and receipt of fare and taxes paid, the other main functions of the standard IATA passenger and baggage ticket are:

- to permit interline carriage of passengers worldwide by as many carriers as may be required to complete the transportation
- to provide details of routing, reservations and fare calculation
- to provide number of pieces and weight of baggage for load control, excess baggage charges and baggage claims
- to provide passenger boarding authority for each sector
- to act as source document for internal and interline revenue accounting and proration payment of commission to passenger sales agent, and electronic data capture and transmission

ticket agent A passenger agent who issues tickets and also deals with the same functions as a reservations agent.

ticket pass See *automated ticket/boarding pass*.

ticketing airline See *airline, ticketing*.

ticketing, electronic (ET) A method of documenting sales and tracking use of passenger transportation and related services without the need to issue a paper value document, i.e., all ticket details are stored in the issuing airline's computer system and made available to those using electronic ticketing (ET) as required so that all transactions, which could be carried out using a manual ticket, can be performed electronically (e.g., travel, exchange and refund). A key term in this definition is *paper value document* since a paper ticket has a distinct financial value and can be given up for the provision of services (i.e., travel), for exchange and for refund.

tour operator A person or entity which organizes, advertises and/or promotes tours for sale to the general public or special interest groups by combining air transportation with surface arrangements. In some designated countries, airlines are not permitted to function as tour operators (IATA Res. 870). Synonymous with *tour wholesaler*.

transfer point See *interline point*.

transferring airline See *airline, transferring*.

travel agency See *passenger sales agency*.

walkway An enclosed passageway between terminal and aircraft for embarking and disembarking passengers. Synonymous with *passenger bridge (PB)*.

wheelchair passenger See *passenger, wheelchair*.

Bibliography

Accessible Air Travel: A Guide for People with Disabilities, Eastern Paralyzed Veterans Association, Jackson Heights, NY, 1998.

Air Carrier Access Act: Common Questions about Air Travel for Wheelchair Users, Eastern Paralyzed Veterans Association, Jackson Heights, NY, 2000.

Airport World, "*Airport Access for All*", December 1999/January 2000.

Airports and Persons with Disabilities, ACI, Geneva, Switzerland, 2000.

Census Brief, U.S. Department of Commerce, Bureau of the Census, Washington, DC, 1997.

Compendium of International Civil Aviation, Second Edition, Adrianus D. Groenewege, IATA/IADC, Montreal, Canada, 1998-99.

Ground Handling International, "*Handle With Care*", November/December 1998.

Ground Handling International, "*Handling Persons with Reduced Mobility*", November/December 1998.

Access to Air Transport by Persons with Disabilities, *ICAO Circular 274,* Montreal, Canada, 1999.

New Horizons: Information for the Air Traveler with a Disability, U.S Department of Transportation, Washington, DC, 2000.

Passenger Services Conference Resolutions Manual, 20th Edition, IATA, Montreal, Canada, 2000.

Tourism for People with Restricted Physical Ability, Keroul, Montreal, Canada, 1995.

Travel-Ability, Lois Reamy, Macmillan Publishing Company, New York, NY, 1978.

Index

Index

Index

                        (continued)